Sex CRIMINALS
FIVE-FINGERED DISCOUNT

MATT FRACTION
CHIP ZDARSKY

THOMAS K
EDITING

DREW GILL
PRODUCTION

LAUREN SANKOVITCH
MANAGING EDITOR

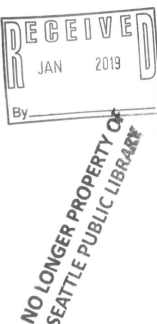
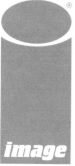

® **IMAGE COMICS, INC.**

Robert Kirkman—Chief Operating Officer
Erik Larsen—Chief Financial Officer
Todd McFarlane—President
Marc Silvestri—Chief Executive Officer
Jim Valentino—Vice President

Eric Stephenson—Publisher/Chief Creative Officer
Corey Hart—Director of Sales
Jeff Boison—Director of Publishing Planning
& Book Trade Sales
Chris Ross—Director of Digital Sales
Jeff Stang—Director of Specialty Sales
Kat Salazar—Director of PR & Marketing
Drew Gill—Art Director
Heather Doornink—Production Director
Nicole Lapalme—Controller

IMAGECOMICS.COM

For Chip,
But not Chip Zdarsky
Another Chip
You wouldn't know him
He lives in Canada
Another Canada, I mean
A different one
Anyway it's not Chip Zdarsky, it's someone else
Siri stop dictation
Yes I'd like seven double monster cheesebusters
Okay sir anything else
And one diet coke please, light ice
Okay will that be all
Yes
That will be thirty-eight fifty, sir
Do you take ApplePay
Yes sir, just tap the phone
Just okay okay one oh wait I think it's still shit shit wait Siri no Siri stop

MATT

For Marvel Comics,
Thank you for the decades of
high-quality entertainment.
You showed me that the
real hero was inside me
all along (The Hulk).

CHIP

21
SPACES

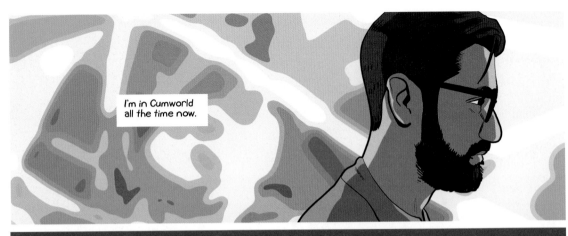

I'm in Cumworld
all the time now.

JON:

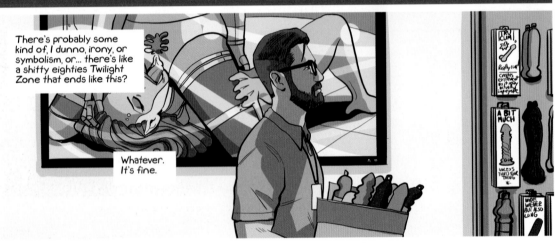

There's probably some
kind of, I dunno, irony, or
symbolism, or... there's like
a shitty eighties Twilight
Zone that ends like this?

Whatever.
It's fine.

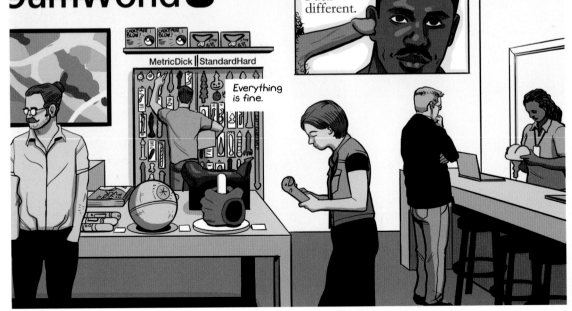

CumWorld

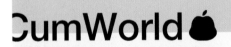

MetricDick || StandardHard

Fuck
different.

Everything
is fine.

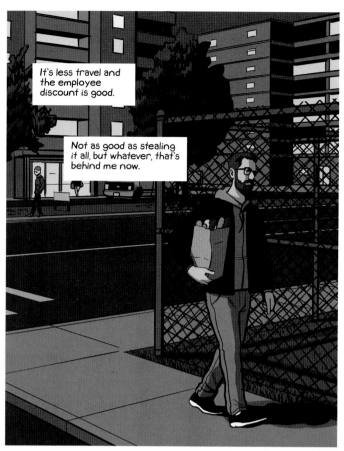

It's less travel and the employee discount is good.

Not as good as stealing it all, but whatever, that's behind me now.

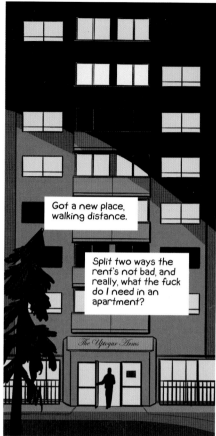

Got a new place, walking distance.

Split two ways the rent's not bad, and really, what the fuck do I need in an apartment?

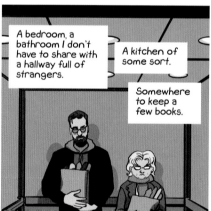

A bedroom, a bathroom I don't have to share with a hallway full of strangers.

A kitchen of some sort.

Somewhere to keep a few books.

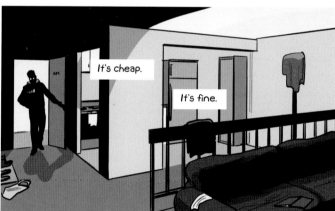

It's cheap.

It's fine.

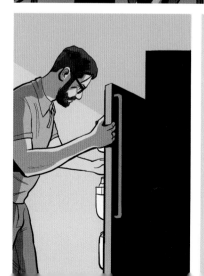

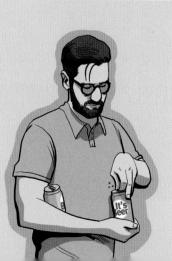

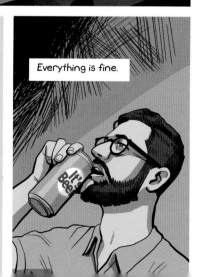

Everything is fine.

BLLLOOO OORRRRRRRGGG GGGGGGPPPPPPPP fffffhhhhh
I'm a little tired I suppose.
Oh hey.
I didn't hear you come in.
Hey, remember that Geoff guy from work?
Mm.
That thing is tomorrow night.
Mm.
Coming to bed?
Mm.
See?
Everything's fucking fine.

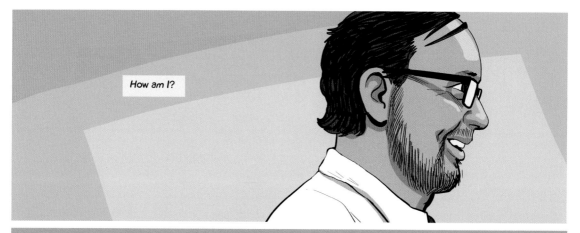

How am I?

DEWEY:

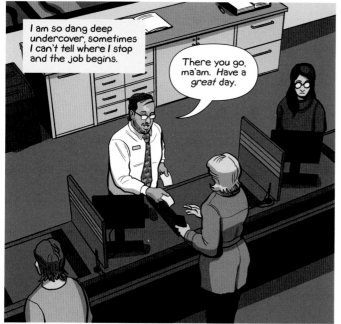

I am so dang deep undercover, sometimes I can't tell where I stop and the job begins.

There you go, ma'am. Have a *great* day.

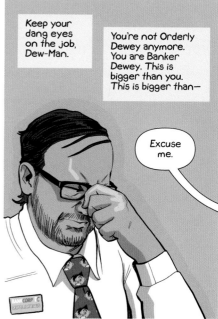

Keep your dang eyes on the job, Dew-Man.

You're not Orderly Dewey anymore. You are Banker Dewey. This is bigger than you. This is bigger than—

Excuse me.

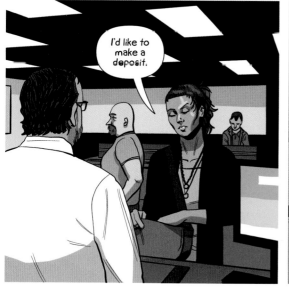

I'd like to make a deposit.

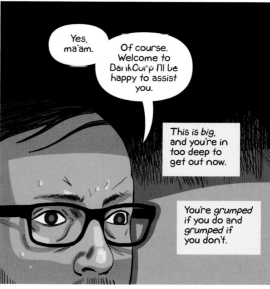

Yes, ma'am.

Of course. Welcome to BankCorp I'll be happy to assist you.

This is *big*, and you're in too deep to get out now.

You're *grumped* if you do and *grumped* if you don't.

FOODGAZI
FOODGAZI
OPEN 24 HOURS
7 DAYS A WEEK
drink it.
Holy cats you guys.
Holy cats. Holy cats.
Thank you.
gdook
gdook
gdook
gdook
gdook
gdook
AHHHH hhhhh.
Thanks you guys.
...Well?
You guys. You guys.
I saw her today you guys.
Yeah?
She deposited her paycheck.
Just like two weeks before that, and two weeks before that.
I'm telling you, it seems like direct deposit would be a terrific banking solution to relieve a little pressure from her busy work and home life, but...

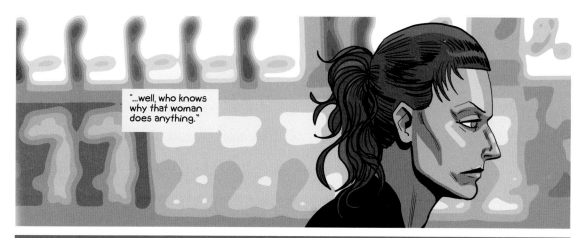

~~KEGELFACE~~ MYRTLE SPURGE:

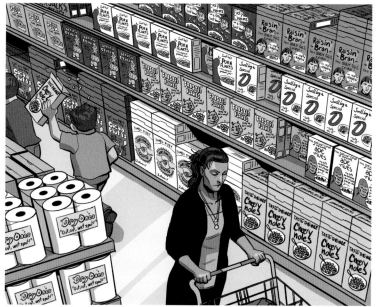

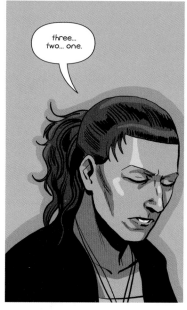

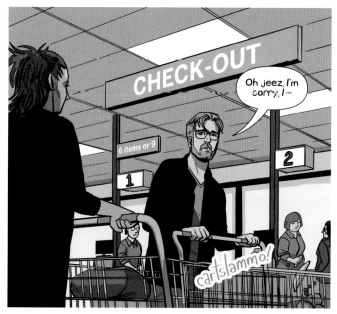

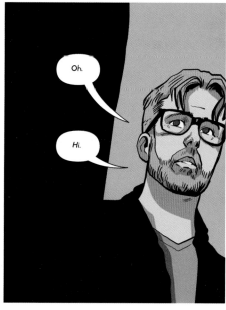

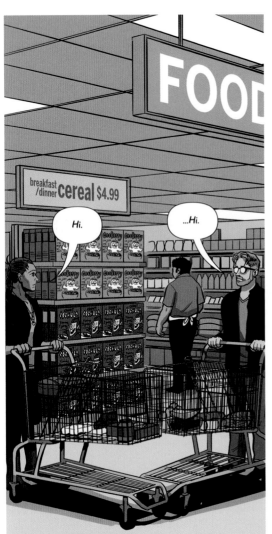

FOOD

breakfast/dinner **cereal** $4.99

Hi.

...Hi.

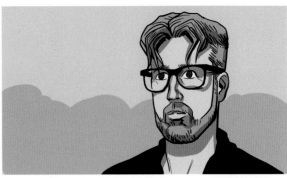

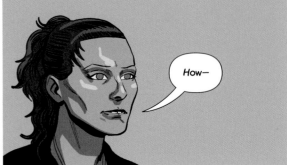

How—

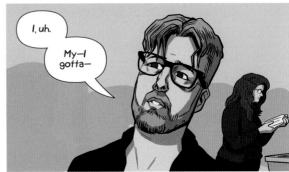

I, uh.

My—I gotta—

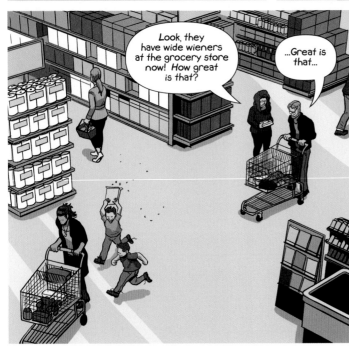

Look, they have wide wieners at the grocery store now! How great is that?

...Great is that...

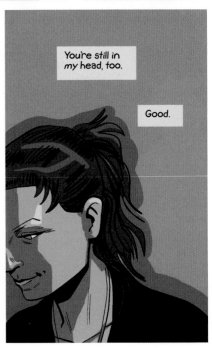

You're still in my head, too.

Good.

Great.
Fancy dress-up party. I know.
Fancy *dress* party, Jon.
That's what I *said*, Pol.
It's—
Hey, I had a nice time.
Yeah, me too, let's do this again sometime.
Oh, totally.
Who's that.
That Becky girl?
Aw, she was cute.
You should see her naked.
Maybe next time.
Seven-thirty, fancy dress, and please don't be late, these are all work people from the gallery and they—
—I don't know, they value this fucking social after-hours yuppie shit in a way I don't get.
Ha ha—okay—I promise I won't even spill a drink on myself and shit my pants before the bruschetta is served.
You're gonna be the only person there I like.
And I'll be all fancy dressed-up.

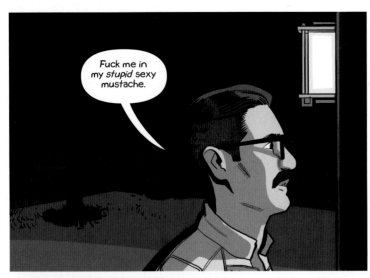

Fuck me in my *stupid* sexy mustache.

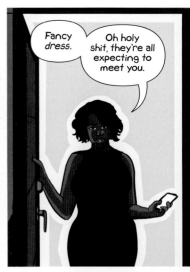

Fancy *dress.*

Oh holy shit, they're all expecting to meet you.

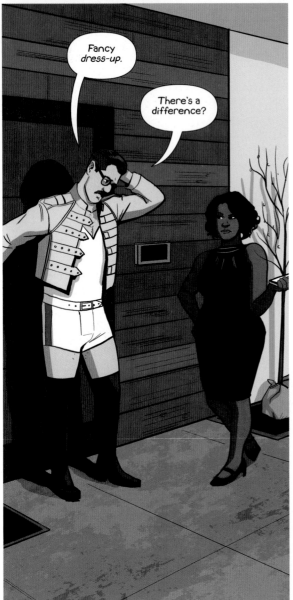

Fancy *dress-up.*

There's a difference?

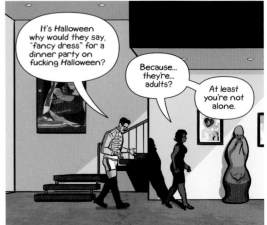

It's Halloween why would they say, "fancy dress" for a dinner party on fucking Halloween?

Because... they're... adults?

At least you're not alone.

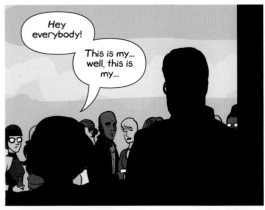

Hey everybody!

This is my... well, this is my...

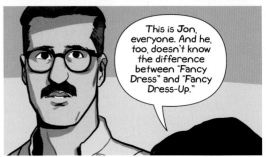

This is Jon, everyone. And he, too, doesn't know the difference between "Fancy Dress" and "Fancy Dress-Up."

Everything is fine.
Really.
Fuck.

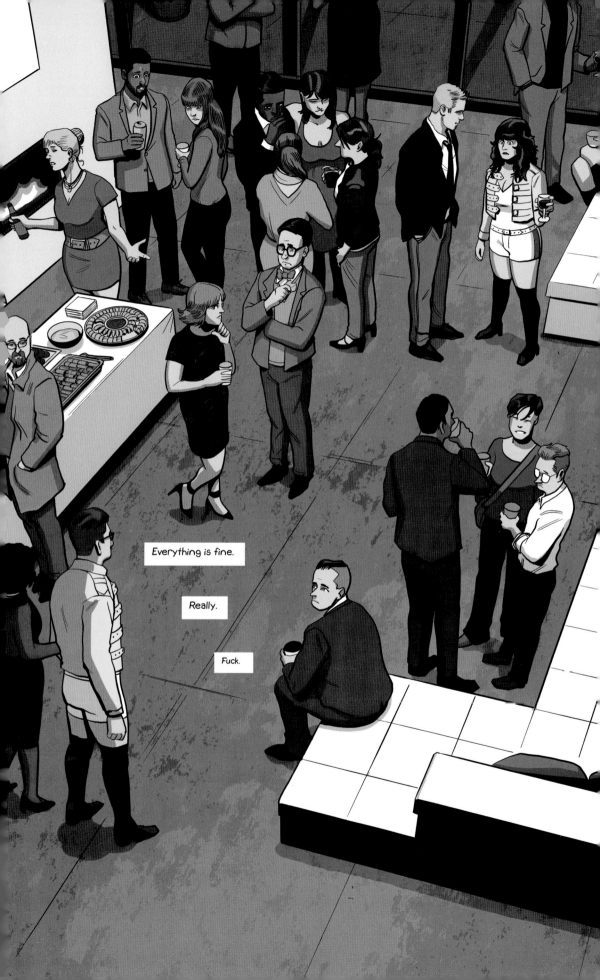

It's funny; it can always get worse.

SUZANNE:

Of *course* he'd be here.
Polly!
Here, come meet Polly.
And of course he'd make the same dumbass mistake as me.

Oh that's funny, you two did the same thing but, like, same-same. I love "Sgt. Popper's Bonely Hearts Chub Band."
Freddie Mercury.
Who?
Queen.
Ha! Just "Geoff." Mr. Queen was my *father*.
wow, really?
Polly is my assistant at the museum.
TERROR

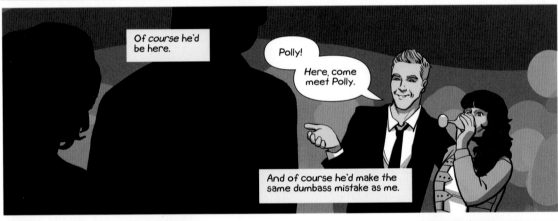

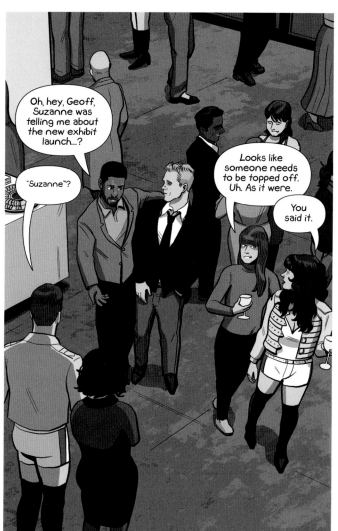

Oh, hey, Geoff, Suzanne was telling me about the new exhibit launch...?

"Suzanne"?

Looks like someone needs to be topped off. Uh. As it were.

You said it.

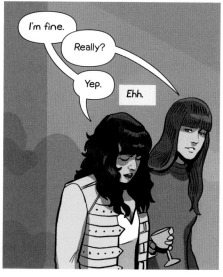

I'm fine.

Really?

Yep.

Ehh.

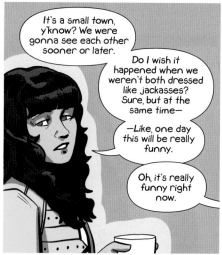

It's a small town, y'know? We were gonna see each other sooner or later. Do I wish it happened when we weren't both dressed like jackasses? Sure, but at the same time—

—Like, one day this will be really funny.

Oh, it's really funny right now.

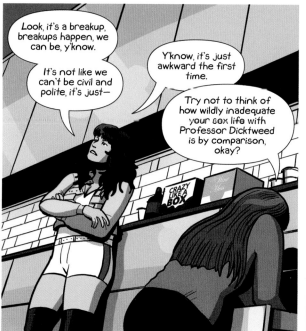

Look, it's a breakup, breakups happen, we can be, y'know.

It's not like we can't be civil and polite, it's just—

Y'know, it's just awkward the first time.

Try not to think of how wildly inadequate your sex life with Professor Dicktweed is by comparison, okay?

CRAZY LIKE A BOX

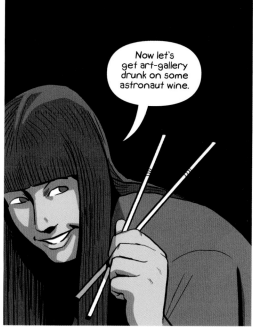

Now let's get art-gallery drunk on some astronaut wine.

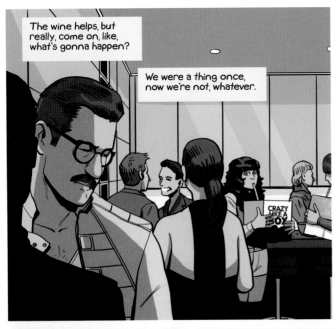

The wine helps, but really, come on, like, what's gonna happen?

We were a thing once, now we're not, whatever.

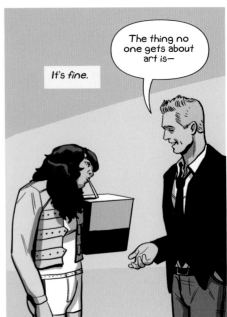

It's fine.

The thing no one gets about art is—

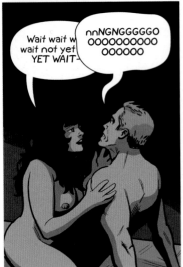

Wait wait w wait not yet YET WAIT—

nnNGNGGGGGO OOOOOOOOOOO OOOOOO

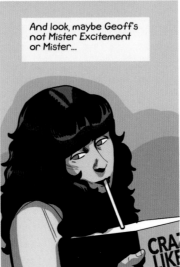

And look, maybe Geoff's not Mister Excitement or Mister...

CRA LIKE

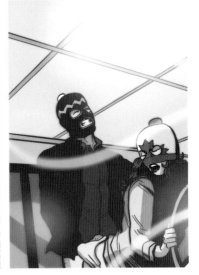

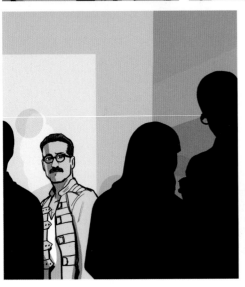

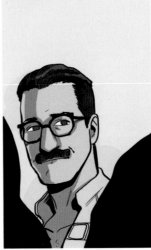

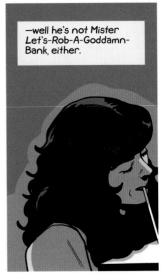

—well he's not Mister Let's-Rob-A-Goddamn-Bank, either.

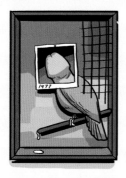

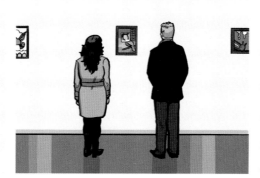

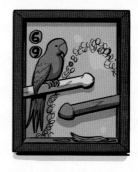

Of course the REAL issue is, what is art, and who makes it, and who decides that art is acceptable? Pornell had no formal training and lived his entire life in the home he and his brother were born in, taking care of them both the majority of that time, and became self-taught while working menial night jobs.

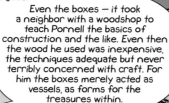

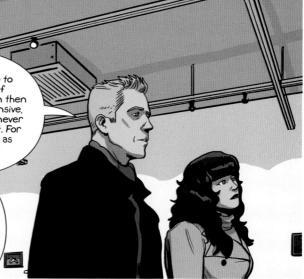

Even the boxes — it took a neighbor with a woodshop to teach Pornell the basics of construction and the like. Even then the wood he used was inexpensive, the techniques adequate but never terribly concerned with craft. For him the boxes merely acted as vessels, as forms for the treasures within.

Why NOT me, Pornell asked. Why NOT these trinkets from the drug store, the toy store, why not this refuse from middle class America? In fact it was this sensibility that brought him into the orbit of Doucheamp, and the two had a friendship that spanned decades, the older Doucheamp acting as a kind of MENTOR figure to Pornell.

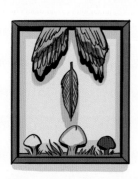

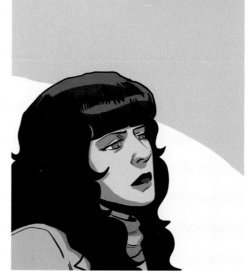

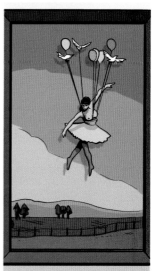

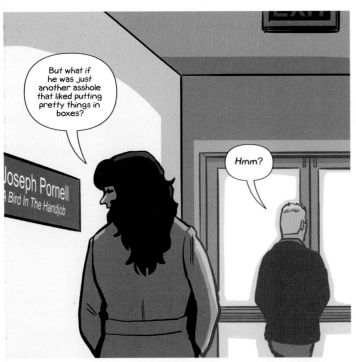

But what if he was just another asshole that liked putting pretty things in boxes?

Joseph Pornell
A Bird In The Handjob

Hmm?

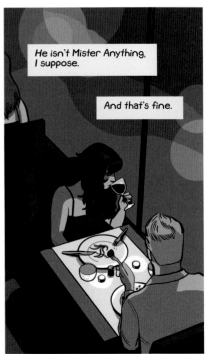

He isn't Mister Anything, I suppose.

And that's fine.

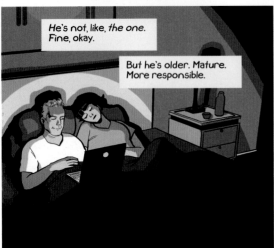

He's not, like, *the one.* Fine, okay.

But he's older. Mature. More responsible.

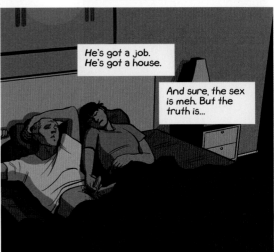

He's got a job. He's got a house.

And sure, the sex is meh. But the truth is...

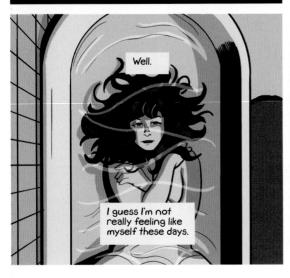

Well.

I guess I'm not really feeling like myself these days.

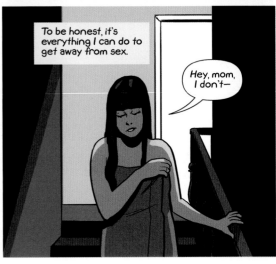

To be honest, it's everything I can do to get away from sex.

Hey, mom, I don't—

Lube
Laugh
Baby! Come join our circle of juicy crones.
We're exploring our deltas of Venus!
Our vaginas!
"So I moved back in with my mom.
"Why?

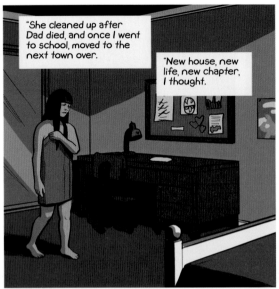

"She cleaned up after Dad died, and once I went to school, moved to the next town over."

"New house, new life, new chapter, I thought."

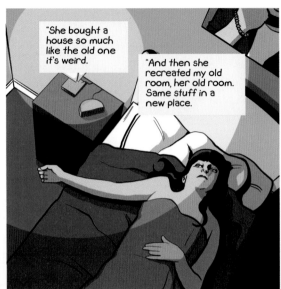

"She bought a house so much like the old one it's weird."

"And then she recreated my old room, her old room. Same stuff in a new place."

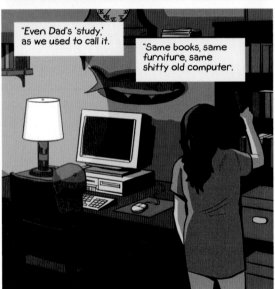

"Even Dad's 'study,' as we used to call it."

"Same books, same furniture, same shitty old computer."

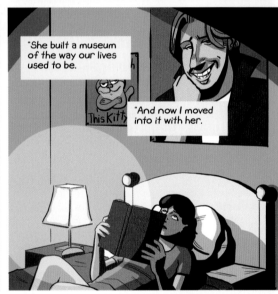

"She built a museum of the way our lives used to be."

"And now I moved into it with her."

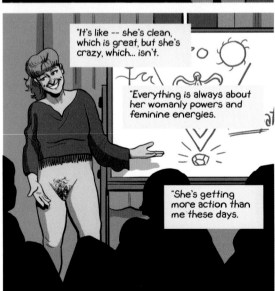

"It's like -- she's clean, which is great, but she's crazy, which... isn't."

"Everything is always about her womanly powers and feminine energies."

"She's getting more action than me these days."

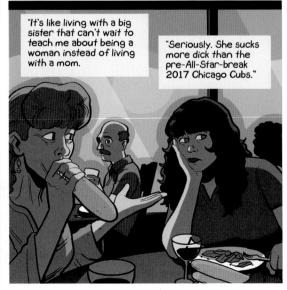

"It's like living with a big sister that can't wait to teach me about being a woman instead of living with a mom."

"Seriously. She sucks more dick than the pre-All-Star-break 2017 Chicago Cubs."

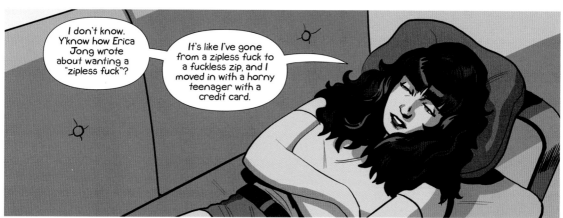

I don't know. Y'know how *Erica Jong* wrote about wanting a "zipless fuck"?

It's like I've gone from a zipless fuck to a fuckless zip, and I moved in with a horny teenager with a credit card.

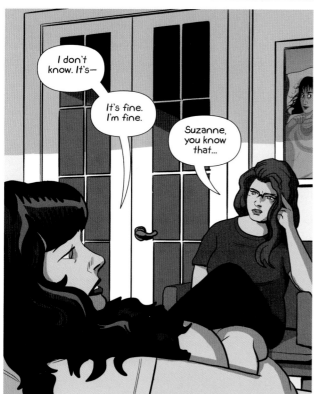

I don't know. It's—

It's fine. I'm fine.

Suzanne, you know that...

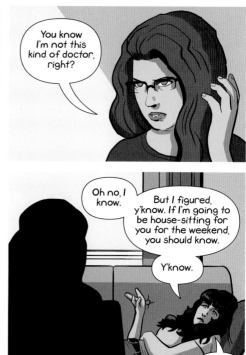

You know I'm not this kind of doctor, right?

Oh no, I know.

But I figured, y'know. If I'm going to be house-sitting for you for the weekend, you should know.

Y'know.

What's up.

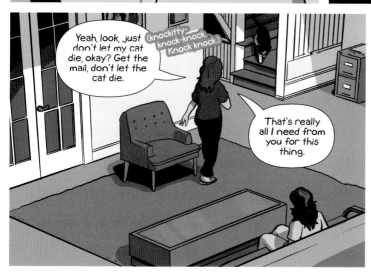

Yeah, look, just don't let my cat die, okay? Get the mail, don't let the cat die.

(knockitty-knock-knock. Knock knock.)

That's really all I need from you for this thing.

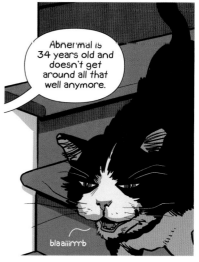

Abnermal is 34 years old and doesn't get around all that well anymore.

blaaiiirrrb

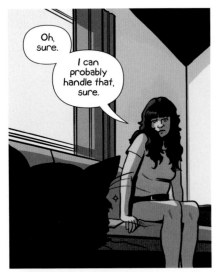

Oh, sure.

I can probably handle that, sure.

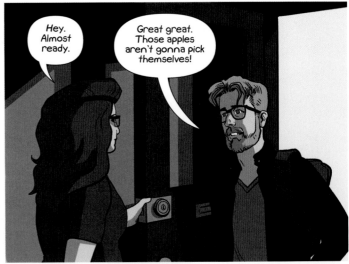

Hey. Almost ready.

Great great. Those apples aren't gonna pick themselves!

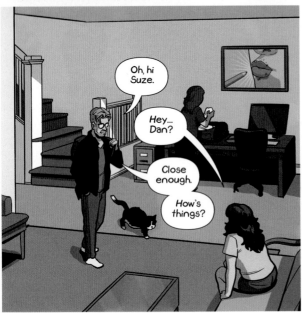

Oh, hi Suze.

Hey... Dan?

Close enough.

How's things?

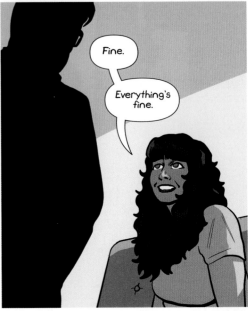

Fine.

Everything's fine.

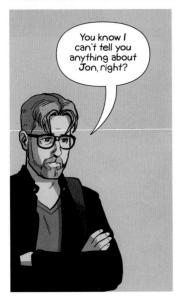

You know I can't tell you anything about Jon, right?

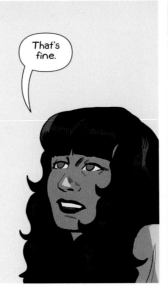

That's fine.

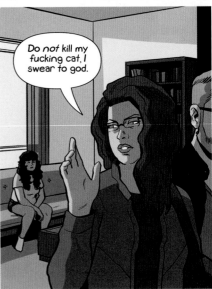

Do *not* kill my fucking cat, I swear to god.

ssssigh.
pllllfrrttt
Oh god.
Everything is so totally fucked.

22
FOLLOW THE HONEY

Okay Momma, I should be back, I don't know, 10, 11.
It's not really that kind of a show, so it shouldn't be too late—
Sweet shit on Gallagher's balls.
But honey, I need the car so I can pick up Mrs. Montrose and Vicky from AA, remember?
GOD DESS

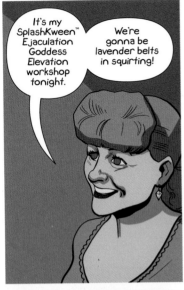

It's my SplashKween™ Ejaculation Goddess Elevation workshop tonight.

We're gonna be lavender belts in squirting!

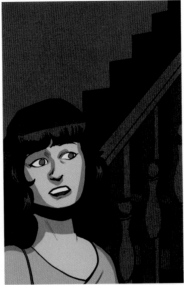

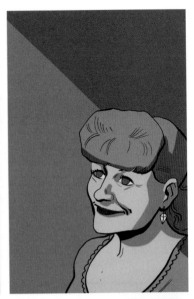

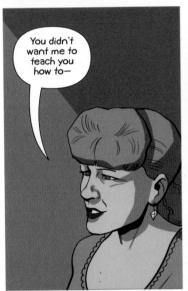

You didn't want me to teach you how to—

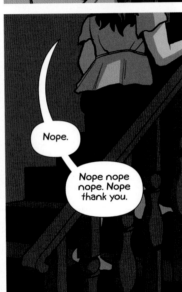

Nope.

Nope nope nope. Nope thank you.

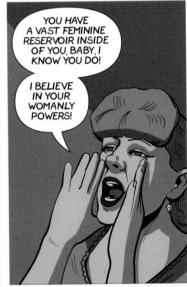

YOU HAVE A VAST FEMININE RESERVOIR INSIDE OF YOU, BABY, I KNOW YOU DO!

I BELIEVE IN YOUR WOMANLY POWERS!

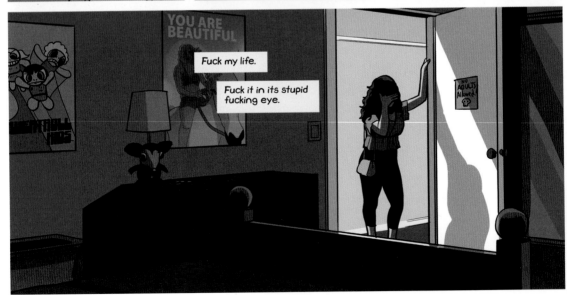

YOU ARE BEAUTIFUL

Fuck my life.

Fuck it in its stupid fucking eye.

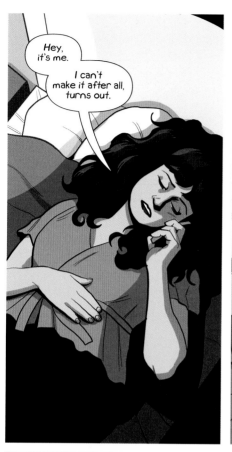

Hey, it's me.

I can't make it after all, turns out.

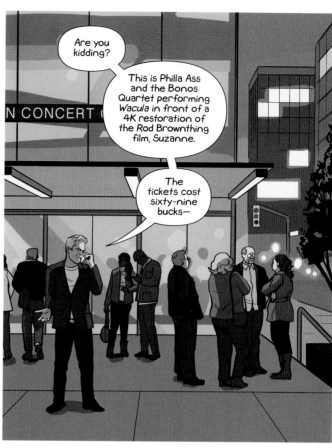

Are you kidding?

This is Philla Ass and the Bonos Quartet performing *Wacula* in front of a 4K restoration of the Rod Brownthing film, Suzanne.

The tickets cost sixty-nine bucks—

N CONCERT

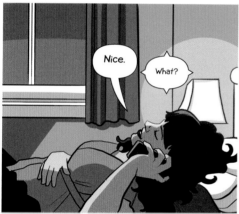

Nice.

What?

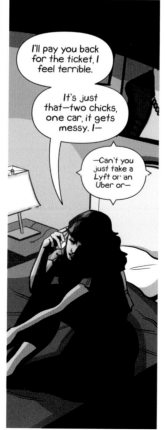

I'll pay you back for the ticket, I feel terrible.

It's just that—two chicks, one car, it gets messy. I—

—Can't you just take a *Lyft* or an Uber or—

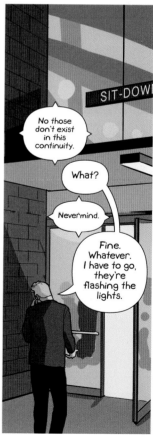

No those don't exist in this continuity.

What?

Nevermind.

Fine. Whatever. I have to go, they're flashing the lights.

SIT-DOW

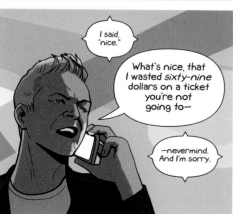

I said, "nice."

What's nice, that I wasted *sixty-nine* dollars on a ticket you're not going to—

—nevermind. And I'm sorry.

Okay. I know. I'm sorry. I—
Hello?
SEXUAL GARY
Don't Mess With This Kitty!
I can't believe I'm back here.
I mean, I'm not back. I was technically never "here."
This isn't where I grew up.
This is my mom's reconstruction of our old life in a new town.
Like living on a movie set.
I have memories that never happened here.
What's it called when you have déjà vu for a place you've never been?
I...bet...that's actually what déjà vu is?
What's it called when your mom expresses grief through alcohol abuse, sobriety, multiple 12-step programs...
...New Age nonsense, infomercial con men, and hypersexualization in the face of menopause...
...while painstakingly curating and recreating her life before the tragedy, but in a new place, in a new town?
Because my mom calls it "home."

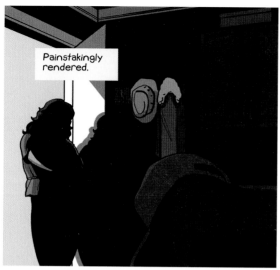

Painstakingly rendered.

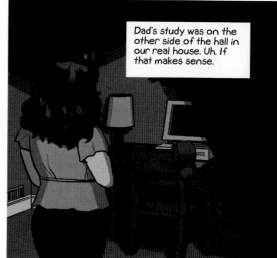

Dad's study was on the other side of the hall in our real house. Uh. If that makes sense.

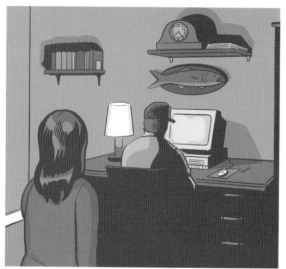

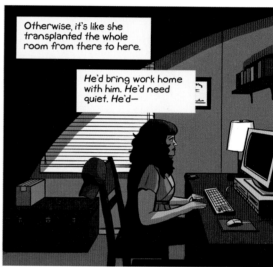

Otherwise, it's like she transplanted the whole room from there to here.

He'd bring work home with him. *He'd* need quiet. He'd—

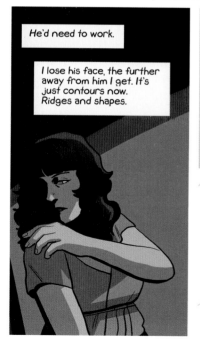

He'd need to work.

I lose his face, the further away from him I get. It's just contours now. Ridges and shapes.

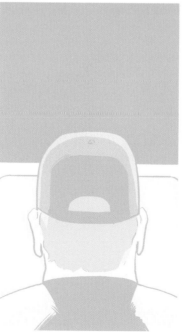

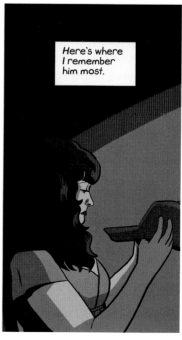

Here's where I remember him most.

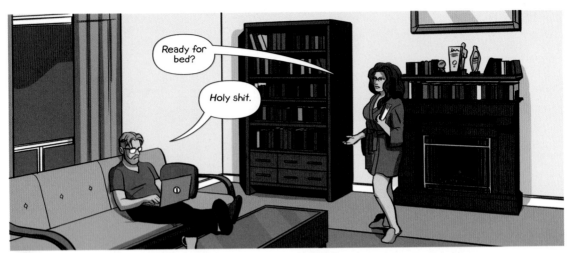

Ready for bed?

Holy shit.

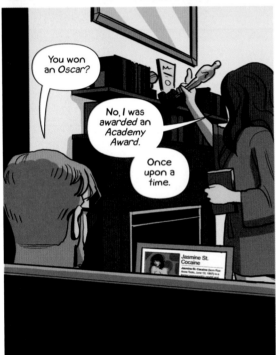

You won an *Oscar*?

No, I was awarded an *Academy Award*.

Once upon a time.

Jasmine St. Cocaine

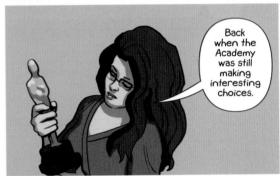

Back when the Academy was still making interesting choices.

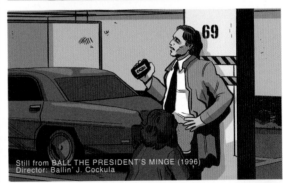

69

Still from BALL THE PRESIDENT'S MINGE (1996)
Director: Ballin' J. Cockula

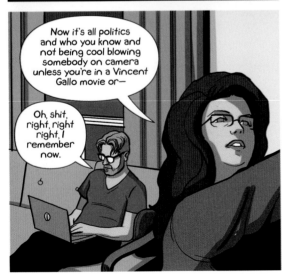

Now it's all politics and who you know and not being cool blowing somebody on camera unless you're in a Vincent Gallo movie or—

Oh, shit, right, right right, I remember now.

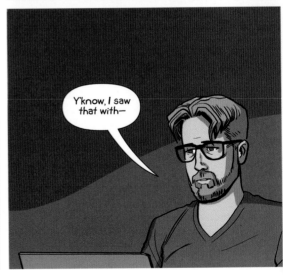

Y'know, I saw that with—

—Oh?
...
You coming to bed, or what?
No, no.
That's okay. No. Got some work to do.
Great.
Okay.

Uh.
What's up?
I'm going out.
I told you this would happen.
I fucking *told* you this would happen.
What would—
Don't wait up.
It's...
It's not you.

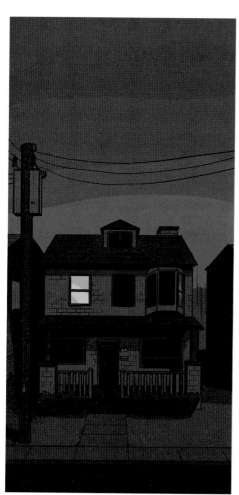
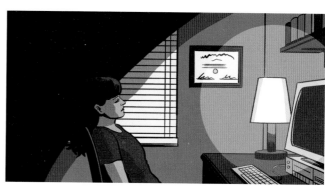
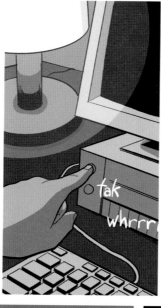
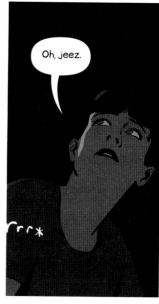

tak

whrrrrrr*

Oh, jeez.

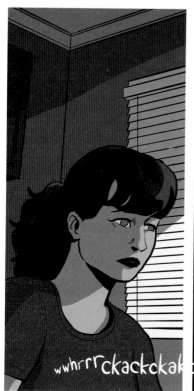
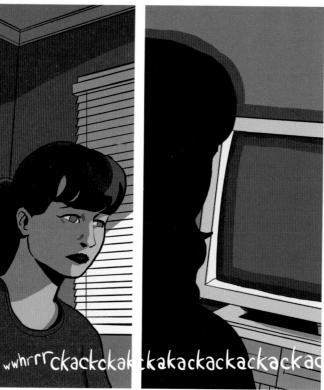
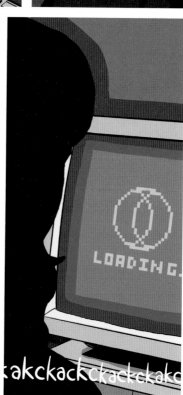

LOADING.

wwhrrrckackckakckakackackackackackackckackckakc

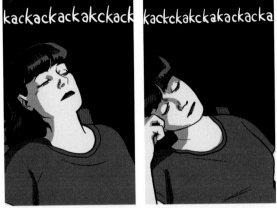
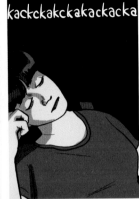
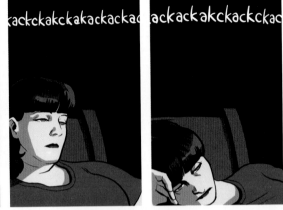
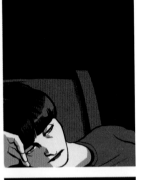

kackackackakckack kackckakckakackacka kackckakckakackackac ackackakckackckac

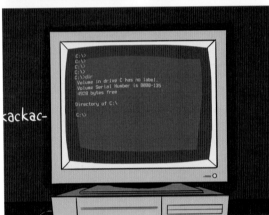

kackac-

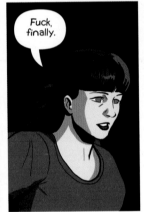

Fuck, finally.

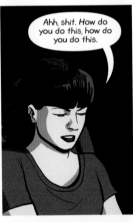

Ahh, shit. How do you do this, how do you do this.

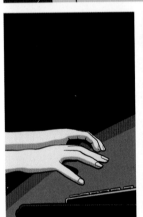

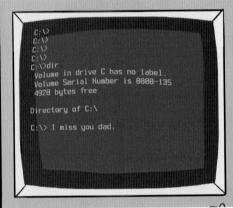

```
C:\>
C:\>
C:\>
C:\>
C:\>dir
 Volume in drive C has no label.
 Volume Serial Number is 8008-135
 4928 bytes free

 Directory of C:\

C:\> I miss you dad.
```

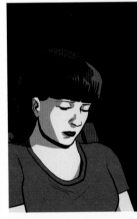

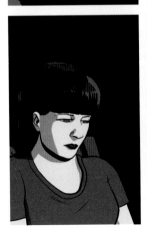

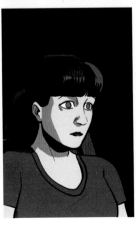

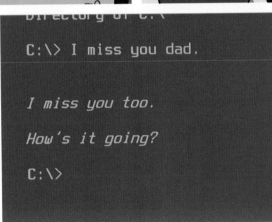

```
Directory of C:\

C:\> I miss you dad.


I miss you too.

How's it going?

C:\>
```

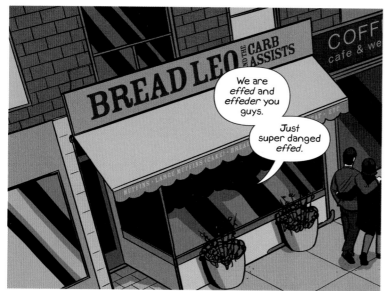

We are *effed* and *effeder* you guys.

Just super danged effed.

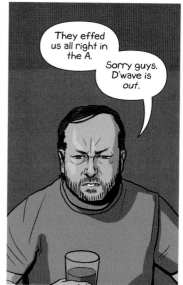

They effed us all right in the A.

Sorry guys. D'wave is out.

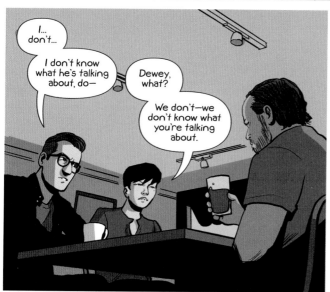

I... don't...

I don't know what he's talking about, do—

Dewey, what?

We don't—we don't know what you're talking about.

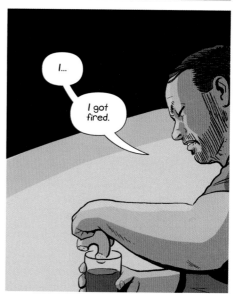

I...

I got fired.

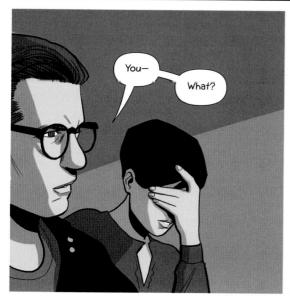

You—

What?

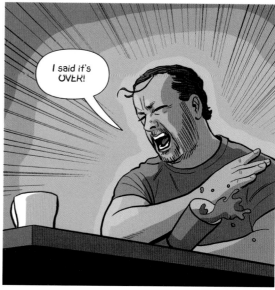

I said it's OVER!

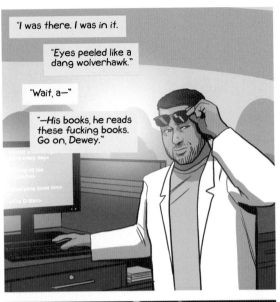

"I was there. I was in it.

"Eyes peeled like a dang wolverhawk."

"Wait, a—"

"—His books, he reads these fucking books. Go on, Dewey."

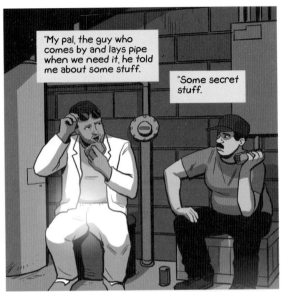

"My pal, the guy who comes by and lays pipe when we need it, he told me about some stuff.

"Some secret stuff.

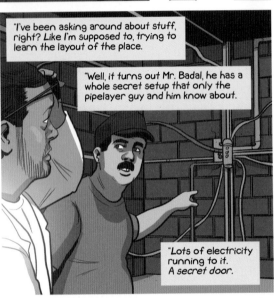

"I've been asking around about stuff, right? Like I'm supposed to, trying to learn the layout of the place.

"Well, it turns out Mr. Badal, he has a whole secret setup that only the pipelayer guy and him know about.

"Lots of electricity running to it. A *secret door*.

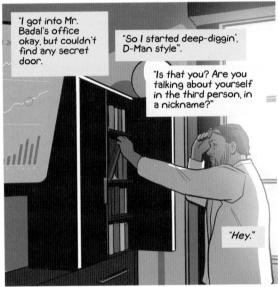

"I got into Mr. Badal's office okay, but couldn't find any secret door.

"So I started deep-diggin', D-Man style".

"Is that you? Are you talking about yourself in the third person, in a nickname?"

"Hey."

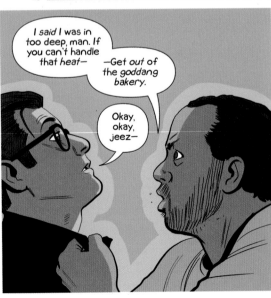

I *said* I was in too deep, man. If you can't handle that *heat*—

—Get out of the *goddang bakery*.

Okay, okay, jeez—

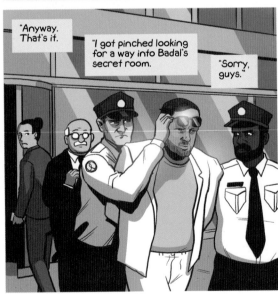

"Anyway. That's it.

"I got pinched looking for a way into Badal's secret room.

"Sorry, guys."

Sorry.
Sorry.
Shit.
Shit.
So...
Yeah.
So...
It's digital then. Right? The files and shit.
We don't know that. Maybe.
If it's digital, if we were wrong, if it's not just paper—
I don't know.
Then there could be, there could be, what, hard drives, copies, a fucking, what, a cloud—
I DON'T KNOW!
Goddammit.
Goddammit I don't know.
I never broke into a skyscraper before.
Now we gotta figure out how to burn down a fucking cloud.

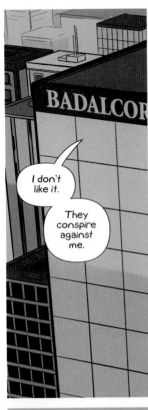

I don't like it.

They conspire against me.

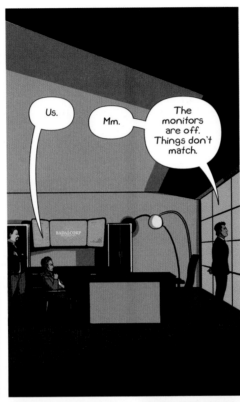

Us.

Mm.

The monitors are off. Things don't match.

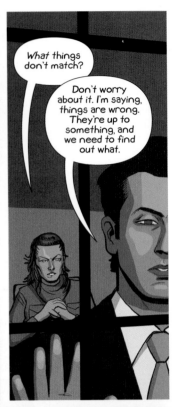

What things don't match?

Don't worry about it. I'm saying, things are wrong. They're up to something, and we need to find out what.

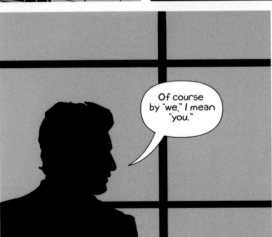

Of course by "we," I mean "you."

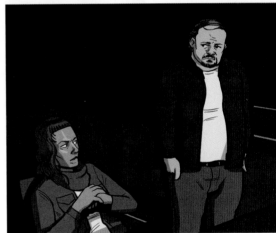

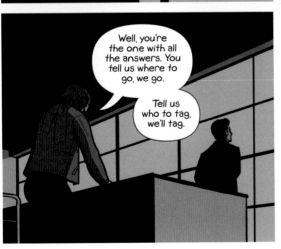

Well, you're the one with all the answers. You tell us where to go, we go.

Tell us who to tag, we'll tag.

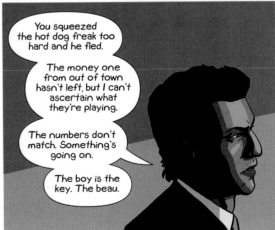

You squeezed the hot dog freak too hard and he fled.

The money one from out of town hasn't left, but I can't ascertain what they're playing.

The numbers don't match. Something's going on.

The boy is the key. The beau.

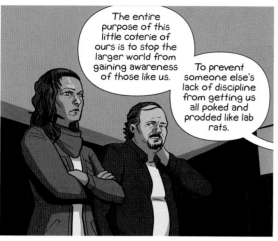

The entire purpose of this little coterie of ours is to stop the larger world from gaining awareness of those like us.

To prevent someone else's lack of discipline from getting us all poked and prodded like lab rats.

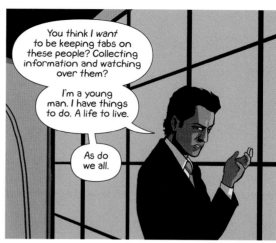

You think I *want* to be keeping tabs on these people? Collecting information and watching over them?

I'm a young man. I have things to do. A life to live.

As do we all.

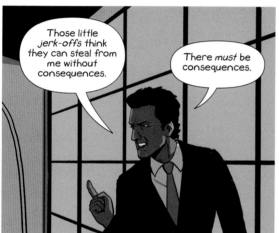

Those little *jerk-offs* think they can steal from me without consequences.

There *must* be consequences.

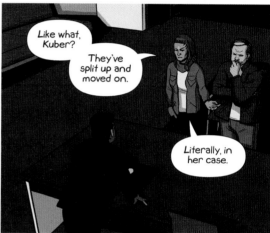

Like what, Kuber?

They've split up and moved on.

Literally, in her case.

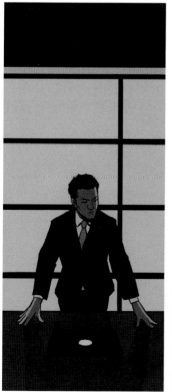

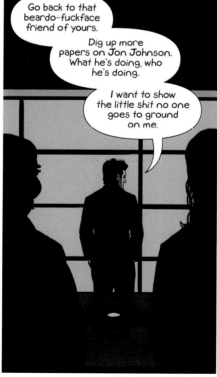

Go back to that beardo-fuckface friend of yours.

Dig up more papers on Jon Johnson. What he's doing, who he's doing.

I want to show the little shit no one goes to ground on me.

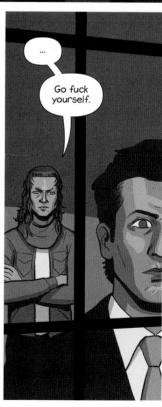

...

Go fuck yourself.

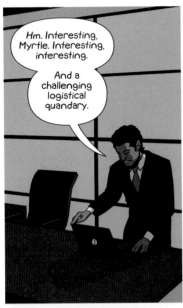

Hm. Interesting, Myrtle. Interesting, interesting.

And a challenging logistical quandary.

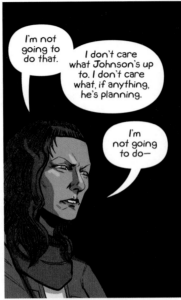

I'm not going to do that.

I don't care what Johnson's up to. I don't care what, if anything, he's planning.

I'm not going to do—

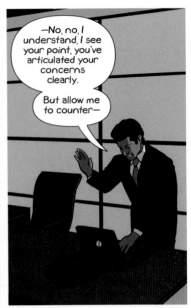

—No, no, I understand, I see your point, you've articulated your concerns clearly.

But allow me to counter—

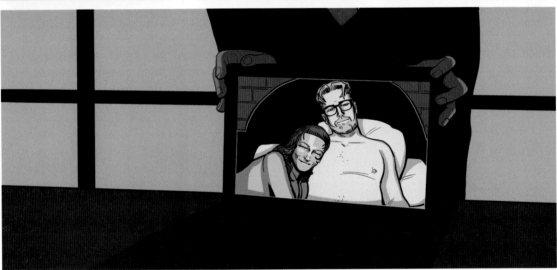

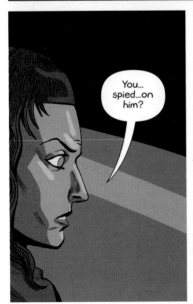

You... spied...on him?

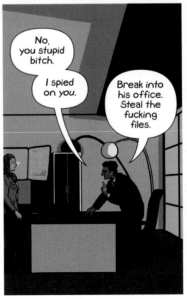

No, you stupid bitch.

I spied on you.

Break into his office. Steal the fucking files.

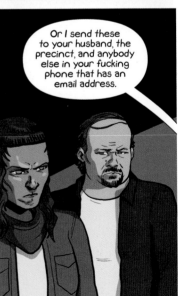

Or I send these to your husband, the precinct, and anybody else in your fucking phone that has an email address.

You with me, Jon?
You're with me, you're still with me, you still want to go here, still want to do this?
I mean, foolin' around with people is one thing, but this is a big step, believe me.
And you wouldn't rather, like, talk about your shitty job or whatever.
We don't need to talk about feelings or anything.
Yeah, no, this is great. I've been here before.
Fuck feelings.

Did I know that? When were you here? I think we talked about that, right?
I dunno, maybe. It was, uh. I was just starting to figure stuff out, I guess.
Angel Vape
And did you?
I guess.
I mean, I'm back, aren't I?
Hey, Polly.
Rudy. We're just gonna head up, okay?

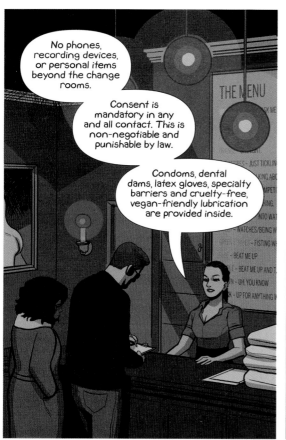

No phones, recording devices, or personal items beyond the change rooms.

Consent is mandatory in any and all contact. This is non-negotiable and punishable by law.

Condoms, dental dams, latex gloves, specialty barriers and cruelty-free, vegan-friendly lubrication are provided inside.

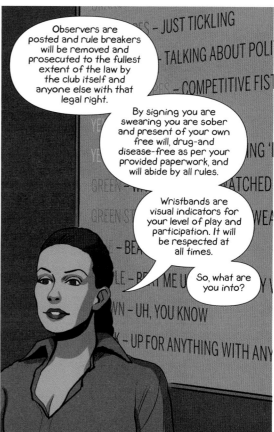

Observers are posted and rule breakers will be removed and prosecuted to the fullest extent of the law by the club itself and anyone else with that legal right.

By signing you are swearing you are sober and present of your own free will, drug-and disease-free as per your provided paperwork, and will abide by all rules.

Wristbands are visual indicators for your level of play and participation. It will be respected at all times.

So, what are you into?

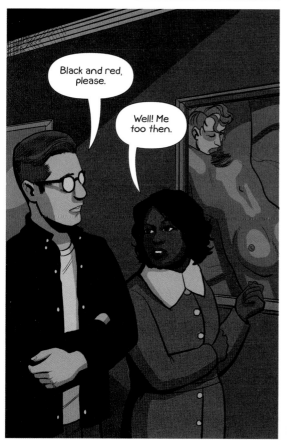

Black and red, please.

Well! Me too then.

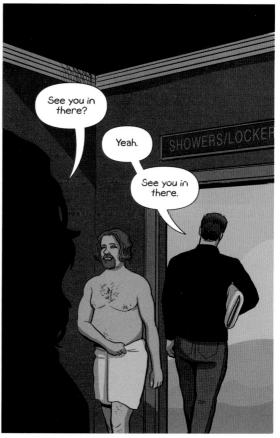

See you in there?

Yeah.

See you in there.

Is this okay?
Am I still into this?
I want this.
Right?
This is what I'm into?
Yeah. Totally.
Okay.
Before was different. I was in a bad place before.
I didn't know what I wanted last time.
I thought you could erase heartbreak with sex.
I'm different now. More mature.
I know what I want.
vrpvrp
11:20
Friday, November 12
MESSAGES
That Fucking Girl
hey you
now
Slide for more

23
MY
EPIPHANY

Ohhh.... boy.
Boy oh boy oh boy.
Nope, nope.
Nope.

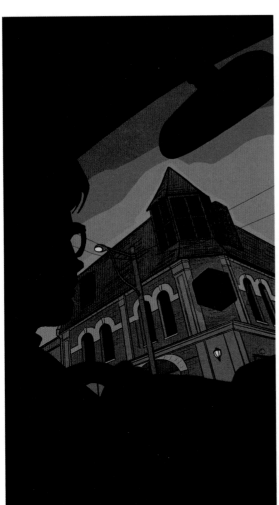

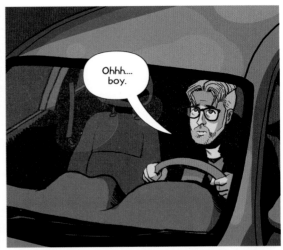

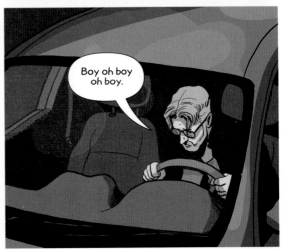

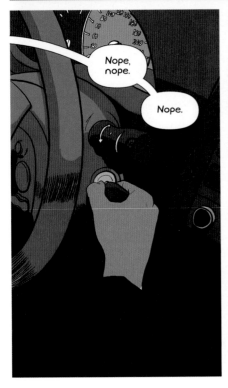

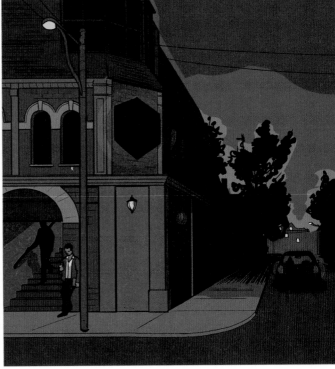

MOM
EATS
DICKS

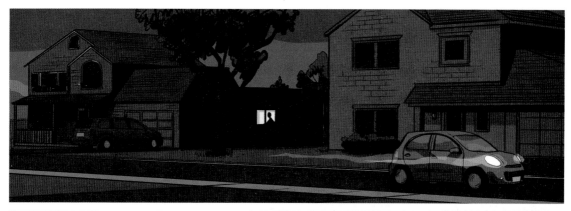

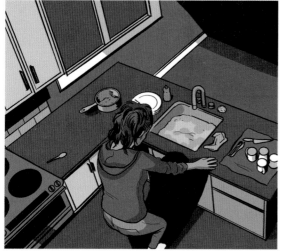

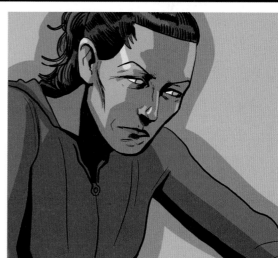

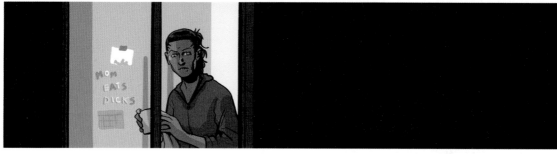

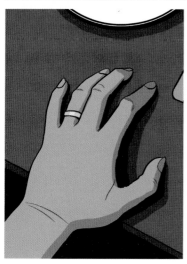

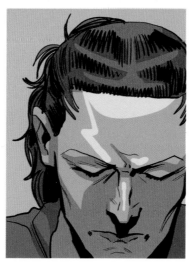

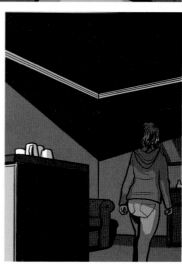

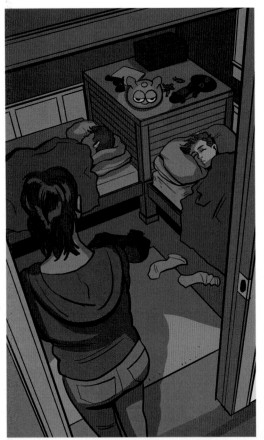
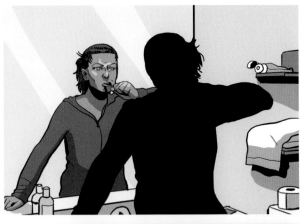
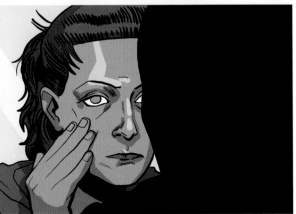
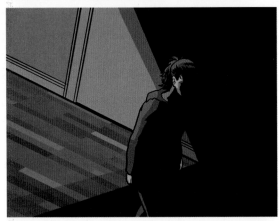
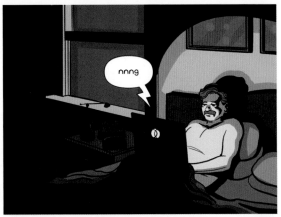

nnng

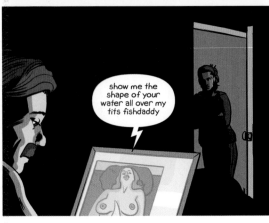

show me the shape of your water all over my tits fishdaddy

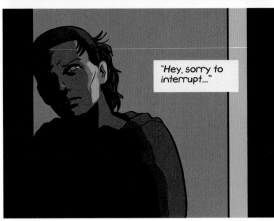

"Hey, sorry to interrupt..."

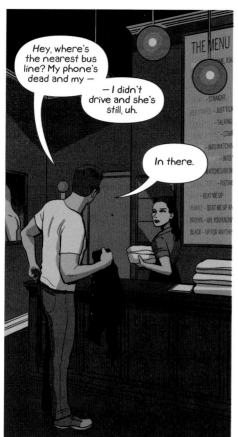

Hey, where's the nearest bus line? My phone's dead and my —

— I didn't drive and she's still, uh.

In there.

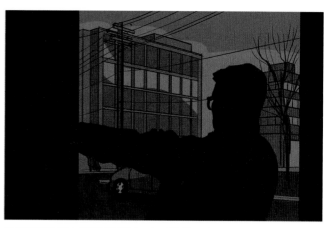

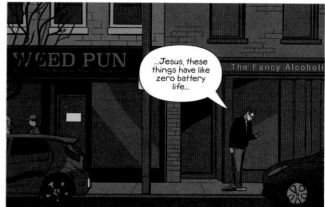

...Jesus, these things have like zero battery life...

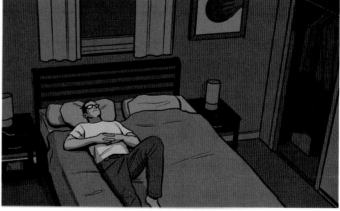

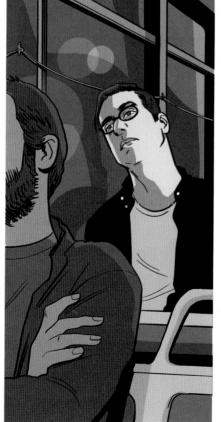

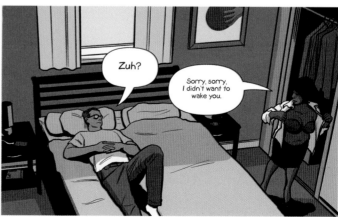

Zuh?

Sorry, sorry, I didn't want to wake you.

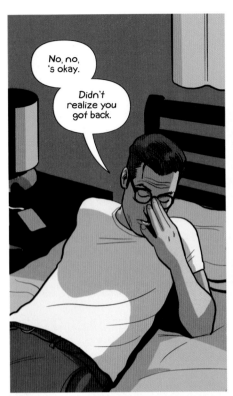

No, no,
's okay.

Didn't
realize you
got back.

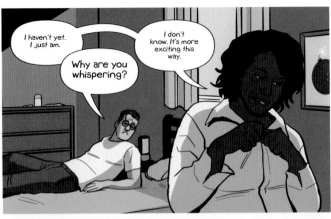

I haven't yet.
I just am.

Why are you
whispering?

I don't
know. It's more
exciting this
way.

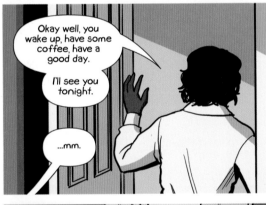

Good
night?

Eh, all right. Kind
of a sausage party
up in there and I
was in the mood
for muffins.

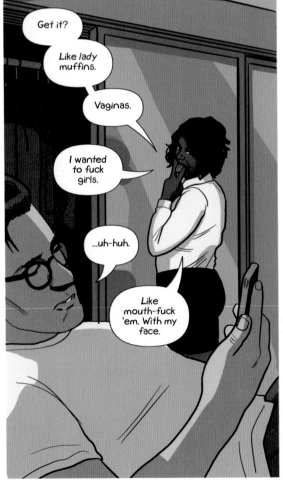

Get it?

Like *lady*
muffins.

Vaginas.

I wanted
to fuck
girls.

...uh-huh.

Like
mouth-fuck
'em. With my
face.

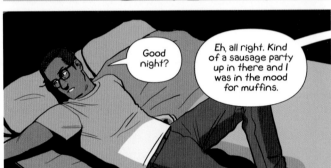

Okay well, you
wake up, have some
coffee, have a
good day.

I'll see you
tonight.

...mm.

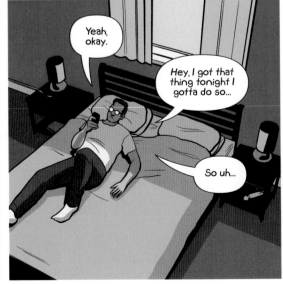

Yeah,
okay.

Hey, I got that
thing tonight I
gotta do so...

So uh...

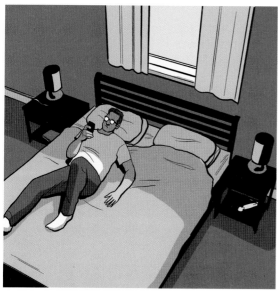

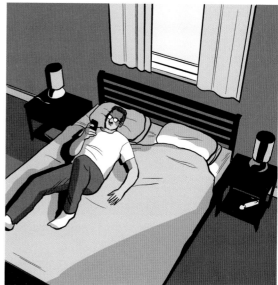

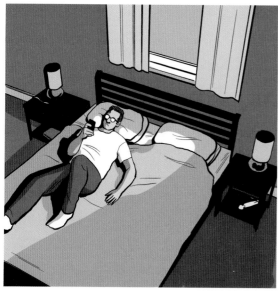

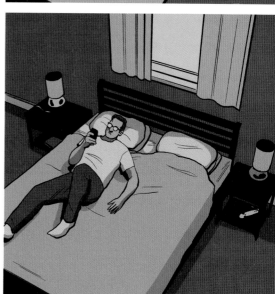

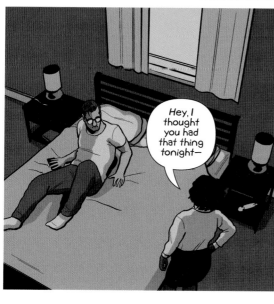

Hey, I thought you had that thing tonight—

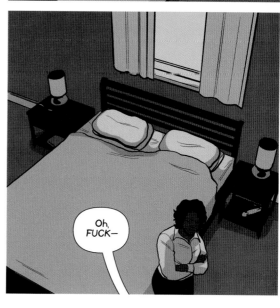

Oh, FUCK—

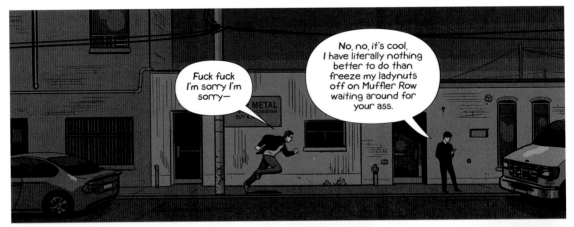

No, no, it's cool, I have literally nothing better to do than freeze my ladynuts off on Muffler Row waiting around for your ass.

Fuck fuck I'm sorry I'm sorry—

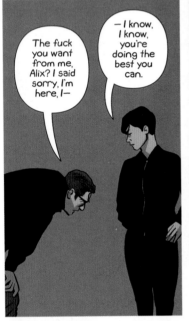

The fuck you want from me, Alix? I said sorry, I'm here, I—

—I know, I know, you're doing the best you can.

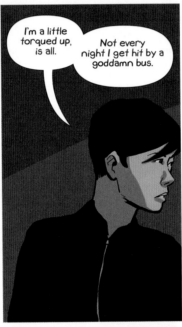

I'm a little torqued up, is all.

Not every night I get hit by a goddamn bus.

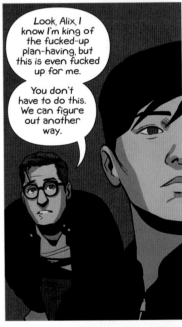

Look, Alix, I know I'm king of the fucked-up plan-having, but this is even fucked up for me.

You don't have to do this. We can figure out another way.

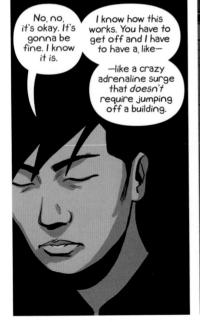

No, no, it's okay. It's gonna be fine. I know it is.

I know how this works. You have to get off and I have to have a, like—

—like a crazy adrenaline surge that *doesn't* require jumping off a building.

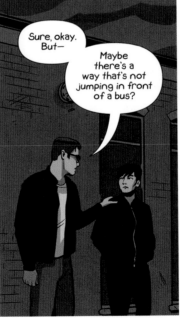

Sure, okay. But—

Maybe there's a way that's not jumping in front of a bus?

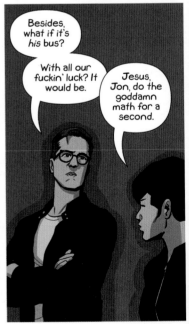

Besides, what if it's *his* bus?

With all our fuckin' luck? It would be.

Jesus, Jon, do the goddamn math for a second.

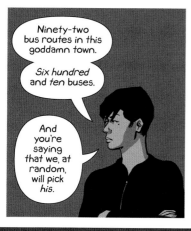

Ninety-two bus routes in this goddamn town.

Six hundred and ten buses.

And you're saying that we, at random, will pick *his*.

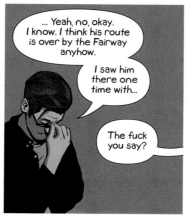

... Yeah, no, okay. *I know. I think his route is over by the Fairway anyhow.*

I saw him there one time with...

The fuck you say?

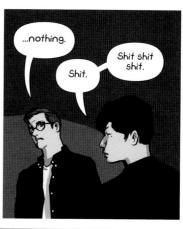

...nothing.

Shit.

Shit shit shit.

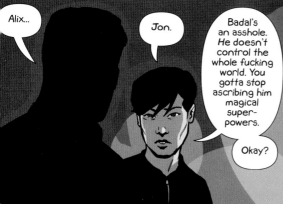

Alix...

Jon.

Badal's an asshole. *He doesn't control the whole fucking world. You gotta stop ascribing him magical super-powers.*

Okay?

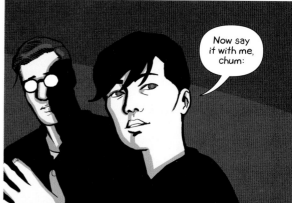

Now say it with me, chum:

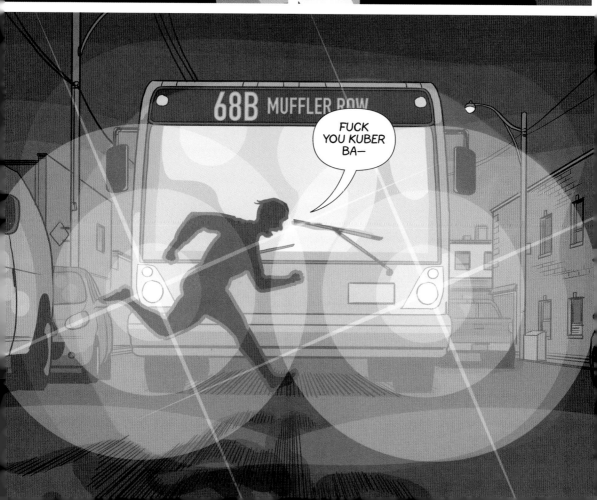

68B MUFFLER ROW

FUCK YOU KUBER BA—

BADALCOR
BADALCOR
BADALCOR

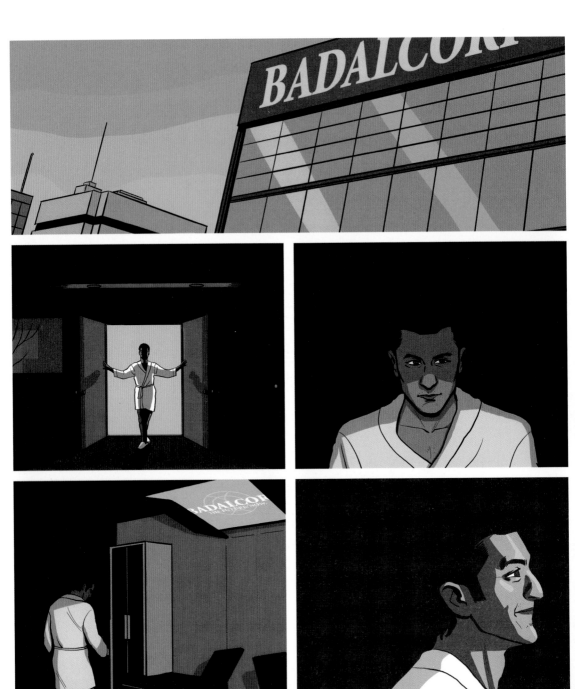

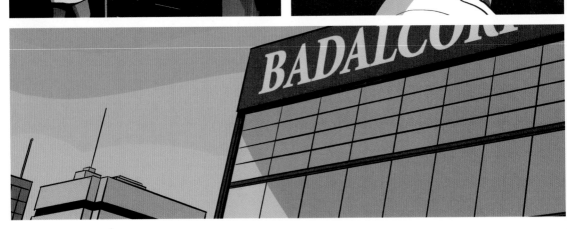

ffsssssshhhhhh
fumpt
fumpt
bddtoo

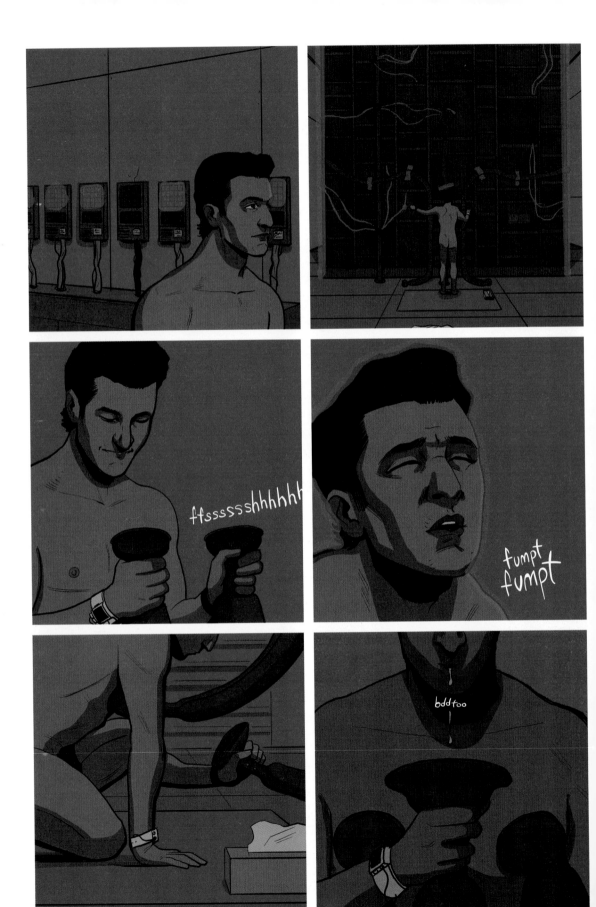

tak
FSSSSHHHH
HHHHHHHHHHHHHH
HHHummpppt.
Aahhhh.
Haahh.
Mmm.

Ng.
Not—
—no god
oh ohh—
nnnnnn
gonna
spurt gonna
pop

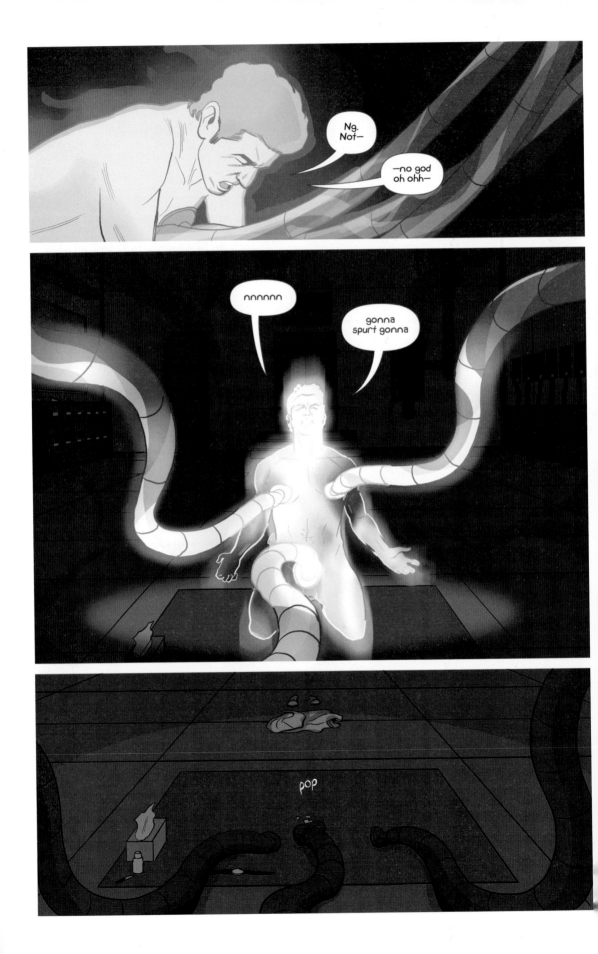

Hhhhhhhu uuuuuuuuugg gggggcckk—
pop
huck
Ghh. Gohh.
God.
Fuh.
Five.
Six.
7:26
21
Okay. Six.
Okay.
P... uh... PRN... 82...
Uh...
OVT 71J
74.8
AKZ
PRN
Shartie

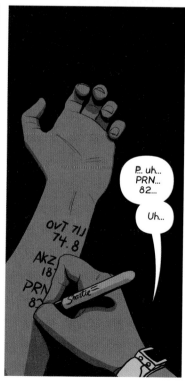

We're buying OVT at 71.1. Short it at 74.8.
That's correct.
AKZ. Liquidate at 19.
Yes.
Now, let's talk futures.
Short futures.
Of course I know the risks.
Six minutes.
Christ, it feels longer.
So much fucking longer.
zzrrrb

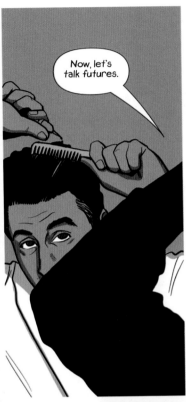

Good morning, Mr. Badal.
Are we ready to start work this morning?
When you love your job, Louise...
NYSEX opening
...you never work a day in your life.

—Hang on—
—not seem to find it anywhere and—
—Okay—
—I tried the computer, and the card catalog, and I even sort of wandered near other books like it hoping—
—Tell you what, do you know the title?
No.
Who wrote it?
Uh...
What was it about?
I haven't read it. I don't know.
What was the subject?
Literature.
It was *about* literature? Like, literary criticism?
No, I'm saying, it *was* literature. I don't know what it was about.
Fictional literature.
...Ohhhhh kay.
What was... on the cover?
It was... blue?
Maybe orange.
Definitely some white?
Jonathan Livingston Seagull.
Yes!
I'm lovin' it.

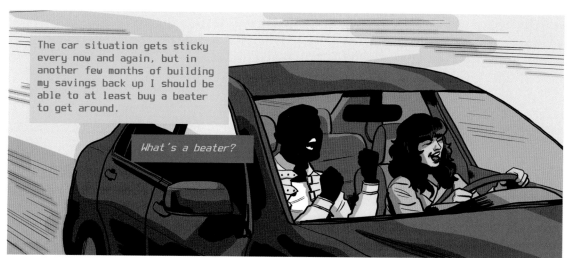

The car situation gets sticky every now and again, but in another few months of building my savings back up I should be able to at least buy a beater to get around.

What's a beater?

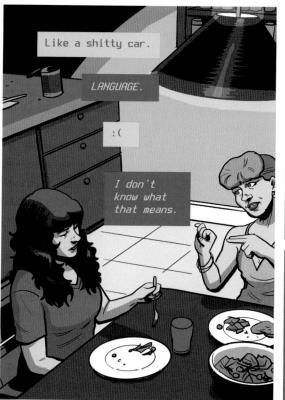

Like a shitty car.

LANGUAGE.

:(

I don't know what that means.

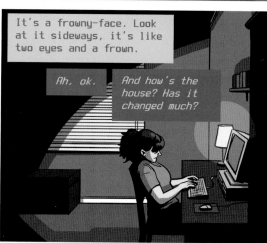

It's a frowny-face. Look at it sideways, it's like two eyes and a frown.

Ah, ok.

And how's the house? Has it changed much?

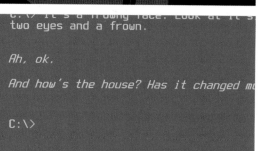

C:\> It's a frowny face. Look at it's two eyes and a frown.

Ah, ok.

And how's the house? Has it changed mu

C:\>

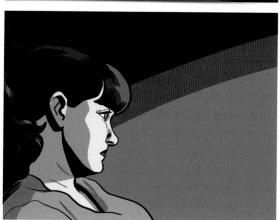

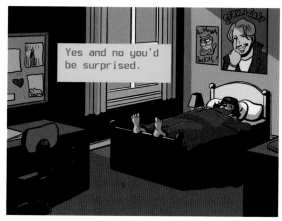

Yes and no you'd be surprised.

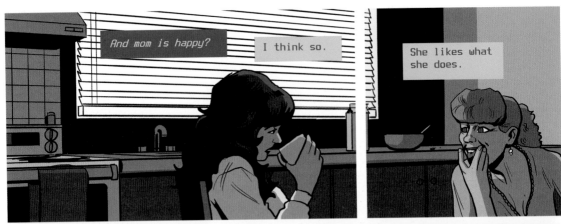

And mom is happy?

I think so.

She likes what she does.

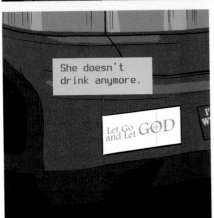

She doesn't drink anymore.

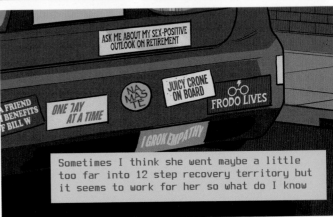

ASK ME ABOUT MY SEX-POSITIVE OUTLOOK ON RETIREMENT

Let Go and Let GOD

I'M A FRIEND WITH BENEFITS OF BILL W

ONE DAY AT A TIME

NAMASTE

JUICY CRONE ON BOARD

FRODO LIVES

I GROK EMPATHY

Sometimes I think she went maybe a little too far into 12 step recovery territory but it seems to work for her so what do I know

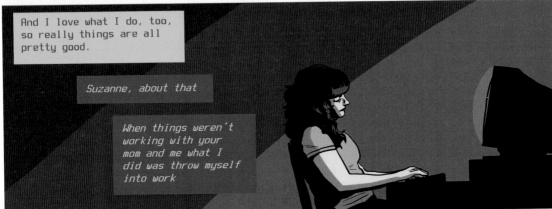

And I love what I do, too, so really things are all pretty good.

Suzanne, about that

When things weren't working with your mom and me what I did was throw myself into work

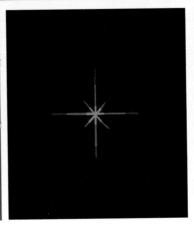

mom and me what I did was throw myself into work

Stuff that wasn't even my job to do, I started doing to sta out of the house

I'm not proud of it and of course I'd do it differently if I could knowing what I kno now, but that's not my point

What I sh|

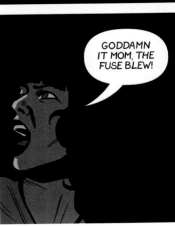

GODDAMN IT MOM, THE FUSE BLEW!

I'M SORRRRRRRRY!
Oh god AWW GOD
I duh— I didn't—
Duh.
God.
Aw god.
I didn't—
I wasn't—
There wasn't anybody in the road or the street or—
I DON'T KNOW WHAT THE HELL HAPPENED!

Keep it together. Keep it together.
You didn't hit anybody.
Anything. I think.
Maybe? There was—
I don't know, a sound?
Nothing on the bus, no marks.
No dent, no scratch, no blood—
No no no noooo—
—Hey.
You okay?

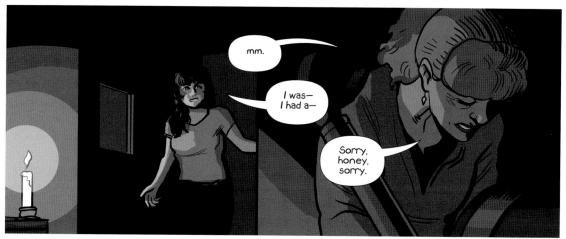

mm.

I was—
I had a—

Sorry, honey, sorry.

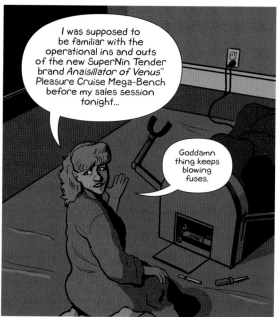

I was supposed to be familiar with the operational ins and outs of the new SuperNin Tender brand *Anaisillator of Venus™* Pleasure Cruise Mega-Bench before my sales session tonight...

Goddamn thing keeps blowing fuses.

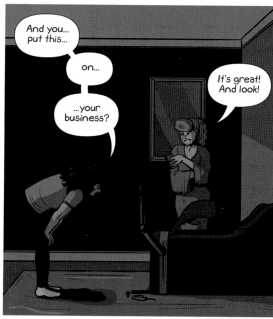

And you... put this...

on...

...your business?

It's great! And look!

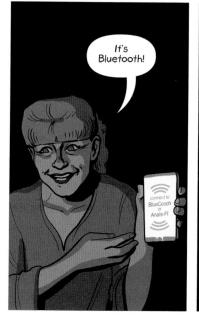

It's Bluetooth!

connect to
BlueCooch
or
Anaîs-Fi

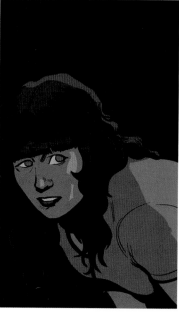

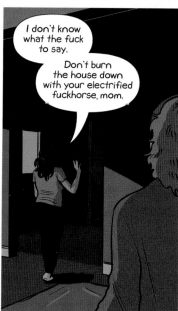

I don't know what the fuck to say.

Don't burn the house down with your electrified fuckhorse, mom.

It's really brilliant, see.

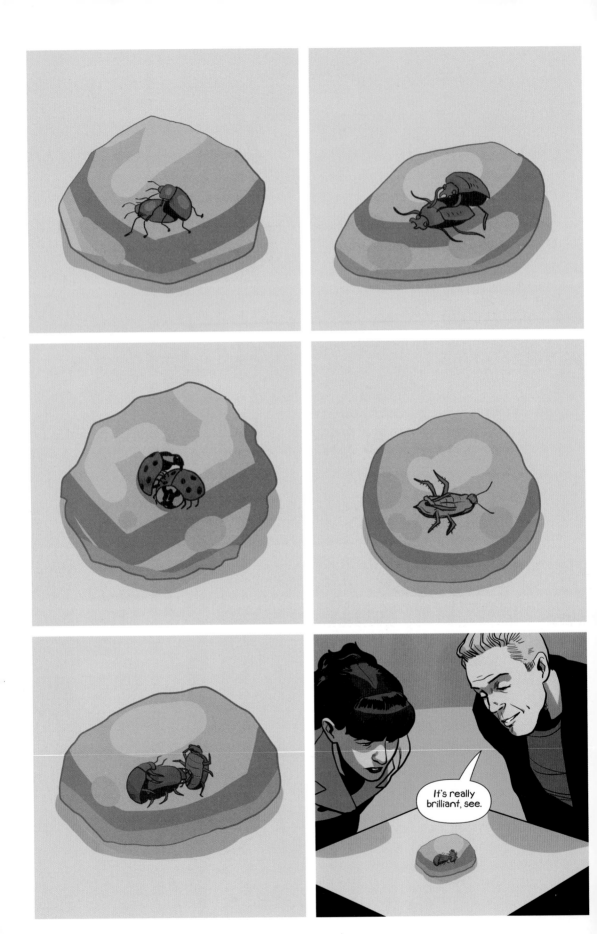

I mean, there's the statement of the thing, and then the, you know.
The "this-is-not-a-pipe" of it all.
I mean, they were all found, right? Not even—
Well, wait.
I thought they were sculpted. Constructed, at least, or conceived—
—Ha! What? No, no, god no.
He buys them on Etsy from, I don't know—
—rock nerds or something—
—then cleans them up a little and sells to curators and such.
"Curators."
One could say he's literally a curator's curator.
One... could.
What else is here?
What?
Who cares?
This is *literally* the only art show in town that matters right now.
Where are you going?

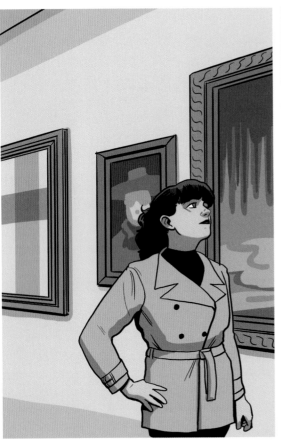

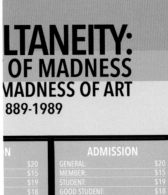

LTANEITY:
OF MADNESS
MADNESS OF ART
889-1989

ADMISSION	
$20	GENERAL: $20
$15	MEMBER: $15
$19	STUDENT: $19
$18	GOOD STUDENT: $18
$100	BABY BOOMER: $100
LEASE	PLEASE HASHTAG US ON SOCIAL OH PLEASE

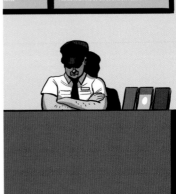

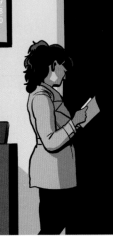

one cannot be removed from the other and we must accept, then, that the simultaneity of both agony and ecstasy go hand in hand, be it through the life and mind of Van Gogh, Munch, O'Keefe, Blake or Bosch.

And these works only hint at what kind of life awaited a more patient, understanding, compassionate world.

Let us close with the words of poet Robert Penn Warren, who addressed his own struggle to reconcile the sufferings of his youth with the traumatic ramifications of his adult life by creating some of the most beautiful poetry on the subject one may ever encounter, "as beautiful as a law of chemistry":

This

Is the process whereby the pain of the past in its pastness

May be converted into the future tense

Of joy.

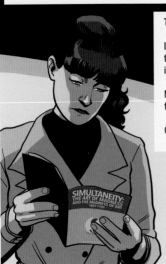

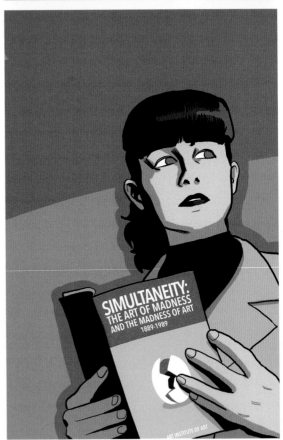

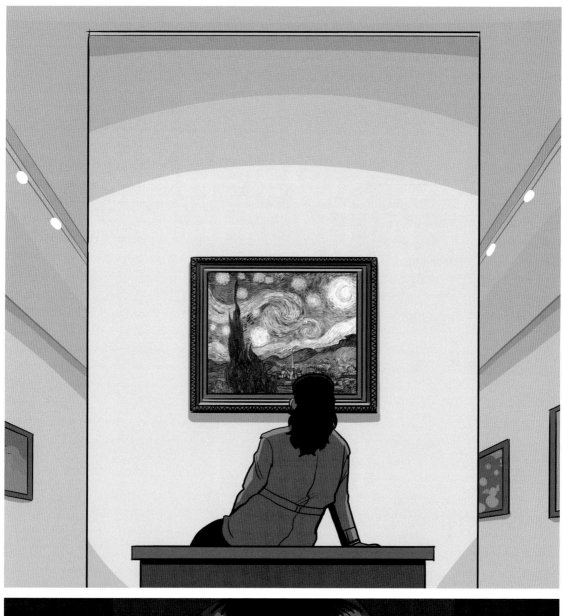

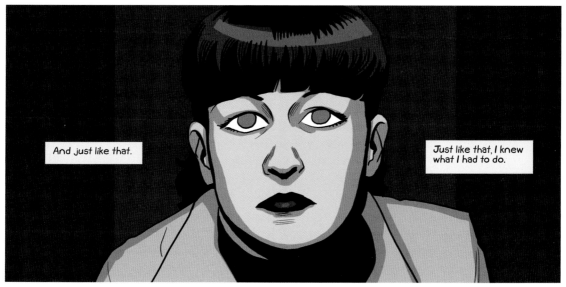

And just like that.

Just like that, I knew what I had to do.

24 WOULD YOU LIKE SOME HELP WITH THAT

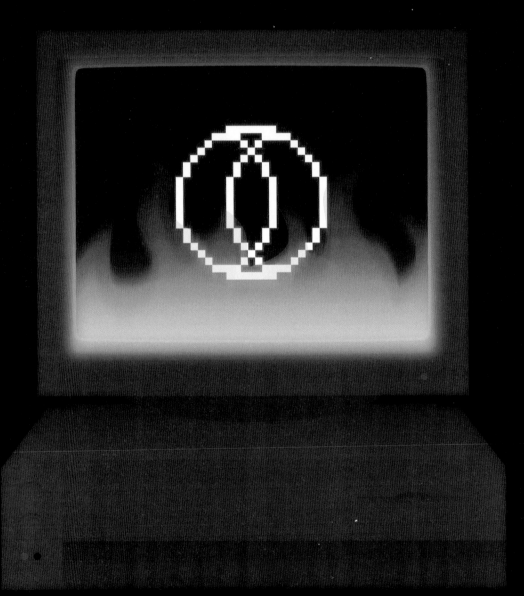

suZANNE!

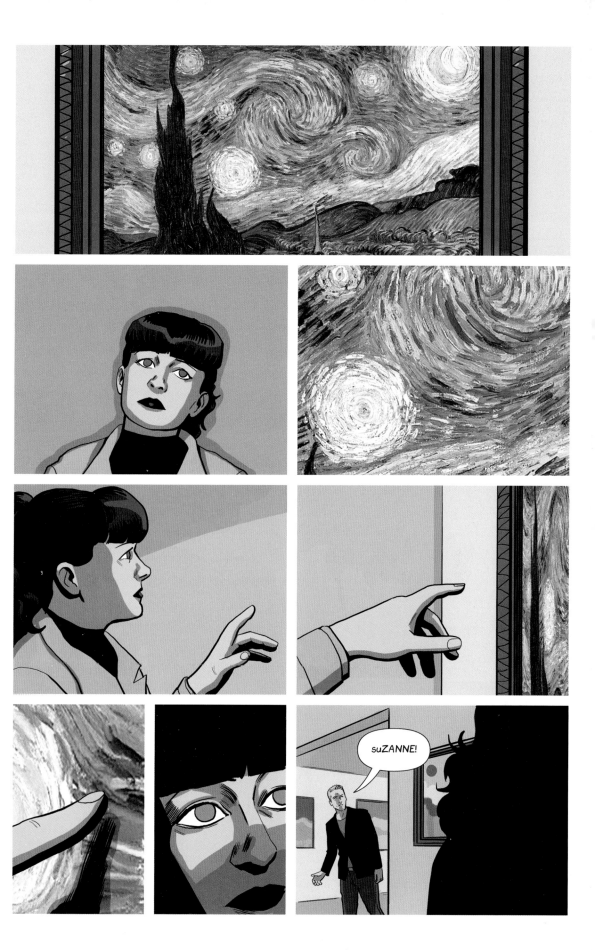

What the hell are you doing?
What the holy *hell* do you—
Shh! You're gonna get me busted.
BUSTED—!?!
You were TOUCHING a PRICELESS MASTERPIECE!
With your bare FINGERS!
Covered in OILS and DIRT and GOD only knows—
—to say NOTHING of the fact that it's not like he's making any fucking MORE paintings—
—and even if he WAS alive, well, shit, we just medicate everything, we just—
"Here young Picasso, have some Ritalin, have some Xanax—"
"—let's medicate the shit out of you so you never do ANYTHING of worth ever again—"
And ANOTHER thing—
eehhh, mah wiiiiiiufff

eehhh, mah wiiiiiiufff
Van Gogh.
You pretentious prick.
...I don't—
eehhh, mah wiiiiiiufff
No, I know, I was—
—And if we'd have medicated Van Gogh, we'd have a thousand more Van Gogh paintings and maybe he wouldn't have killed himself in goddamn agony.
eehhh, mah wiiiiiiufff
eehhh, mah wiiiiiiufff
I can't *believe* you left your *ringer* on in a gallery.
EXIT
Oh, fuck you.
eehhh, mah wiiiiiiufff

([Bug]
(Fuck])
Insects
In Time And
Coitus
Fugbuck
P. Interest, PhD
Major Works
Oh my god.
Oh my god.

BRIMPR
8:46 PM
Messages
ThatFucking Guy
Options
Yesterday
hey you
Today
sorry missed this
poopin
hey

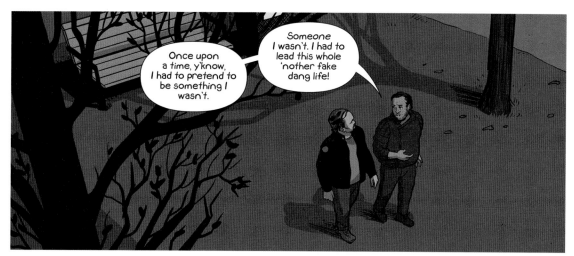

Once upon a time, y'know, I had to pretend to be something I wasn't.

Someone I wasn't. I had to lead this whole 'nother fake dang life!

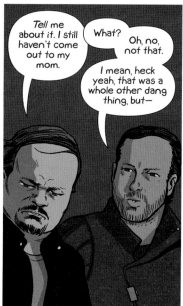

Tell me about it. I still haven't come out to my mom.

What?

Oh, no, not that.

I mean, heck yeah, that was a whole other dang thing, but—

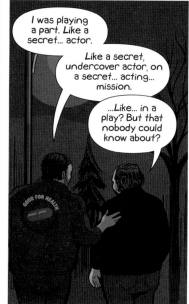

I was playing a part. Like a secret... actor.

Like a secret, undercover actor, on a secret... acting... mission.

...Like... in a play? But that nobody could know about?

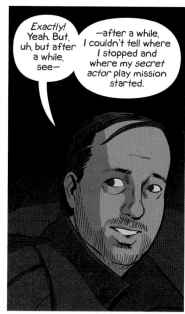

Exactly! Yeah. But, uh, but after a while, see—

—after a while, I couldn't tell where I stopped and where my *secret actor* play mission started.

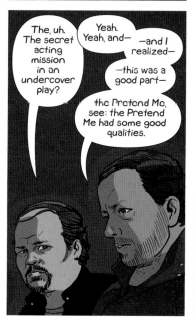

The, uh. The secret acting mission in an undercover play?

Yeah. Yeah, and—

—and I realized—

—this was a good part—

the Pretend Me, see: the Pretend Me had some good qualities.

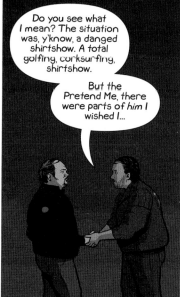

Do you see what I mean? The situation was, y'know, a danged shirtshow. A total golfing, corksurfing, shirtshow.

But the Pretend Me, there were parts of *him* I wished I...

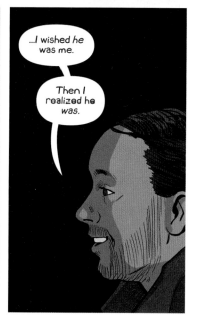

...I wished *he* was me.

Then I realized he *was*.

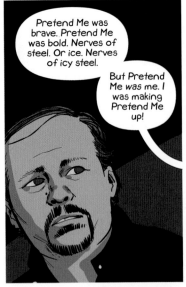

Pretend Me was brave. Pretend Me was bold. Nerves of steel. Or ice. Nerves of icy steel.

But Pretend Me *was* me. I was making Pretend Me up!

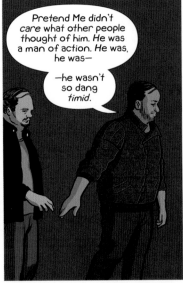

Pretend Me didn't *care* what other people thought of him. He was a man of action. He was, he was—

—he wasn't so dang *timid*.

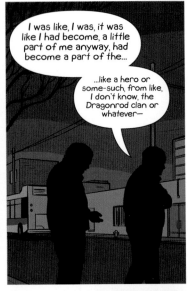

I was like, I was, it was like I had become, a little part of me anyway, had become a part of the...

...like a hero or some-such, from like, I don't know, the Dragonrod clan or whatever—

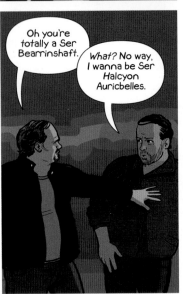

Oh you're totally a Ser Bearrinshaft.

What? No way, I wanna be Ser Halcyon Auricbelles.

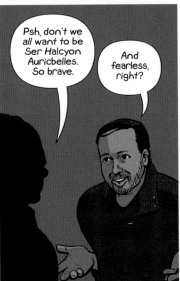

Psh, don't we *all* want to be Ser Halcyon Auricbelles. So brave.

And fearless, right?

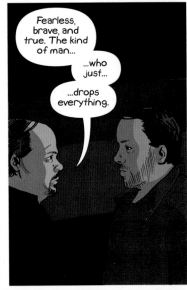

Fearless, brave, and true. The kind of man...

...who just...

...drops everything.

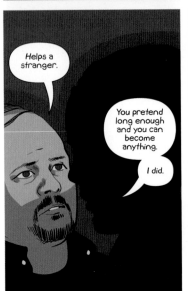

Helps a stranger.

You pretend long enough and you can become anything.

I did.

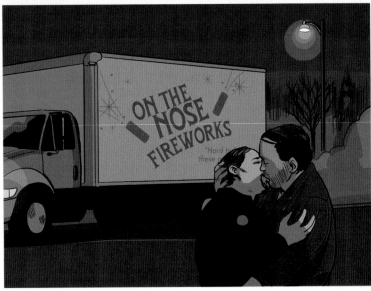

ON THE NOSE FIREWORKS

"Hard to
these

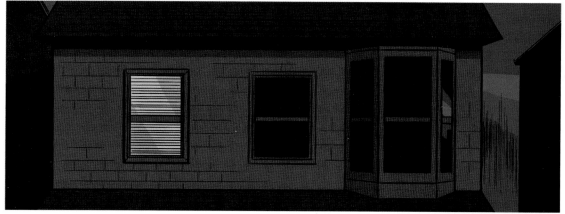

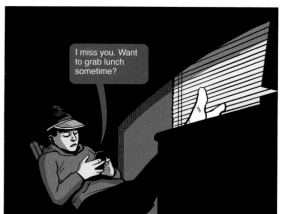

I miss you. Want to grab lunch sometime?

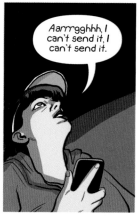

Aarrrgghhh, I can't send it, I can't send it.

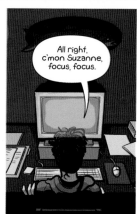

All right, c'mon Suzanne, focus, focus.

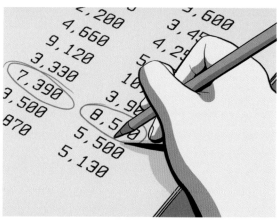

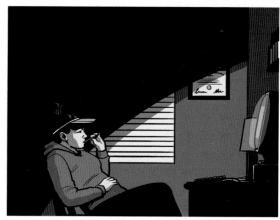

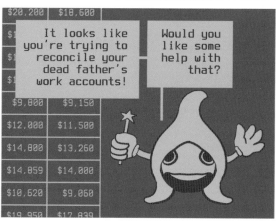

It looks like you're trying to reconcile your dead father's work accounts!

Would you like some help with that?

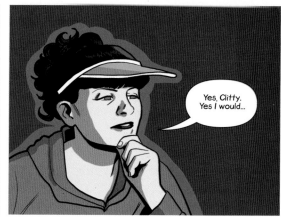

Yes, Clitty. Yes I would...

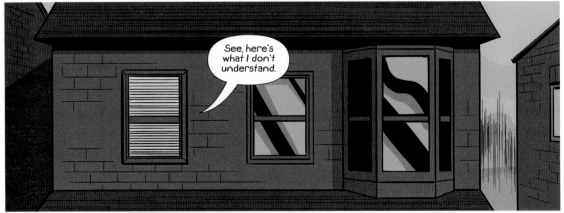

See, here's what I don't understand.

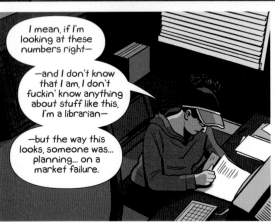

I mean, if I'm looking at these numbers right—

—and I don't know that I am, I don't fuckin' know anything about stuff like this, I'm a librarian—

—but the way this looks, someone was... planning... on a market failure.

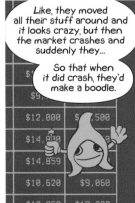

Like, they moved all their stuff around and it looks crazy, but then the market crashes and suddenly they...

So that when it did crash, they'd make a boodle.

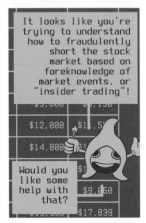

It looks like you're trying to understand how to fraudulently short the stock market based on foreknowledge of market events, or "insider trading"!

Would you like some help with that?

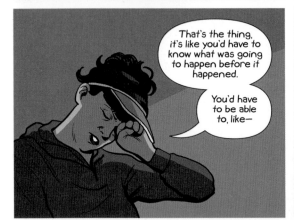

That's the thing, it's like you'd have to know what was going to happen before it happened.

You'd have to be able to, like—

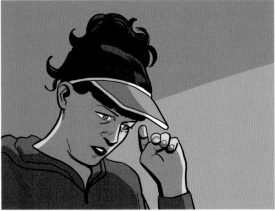

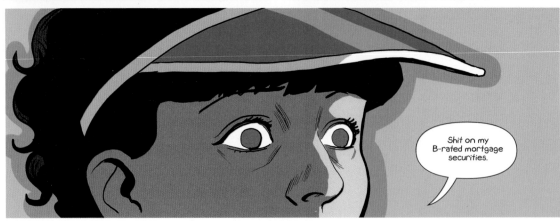

Shit on my B-rated mortgage securities.

No no no no no.
#94-8 5987-14238
ING
23-33
14238...
14238, 14238...
It looks like you're about to put together a decades-long financial conspiracy that radiates tragedy and catastrophe upon your life at various stages and intervals!
Would you like some help with that?
Mother *fuck*.
ACCOUNT #94-8 5987-14238
BADAL, KUBER SINGH
1619 Madorow Ave
Appletown
G86P2P
ACCOUNT #94-8 5987-14238
BADAL, KUBER SINGH
1619 Madorow Ave
Appletown
G86P2P

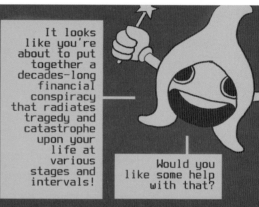

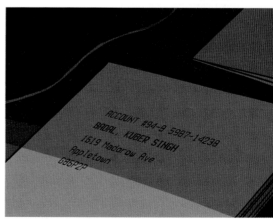

GODDAMMIT, MOM!
God dammit god dammit.
I miss you. Want to grab lunch sometime?
sending sound
Goddamn monster vibrator fucking fuse box piece of shit—
SUZANNNNNE!
Holy SHIT—
—Baby, get out of the house now now GO—

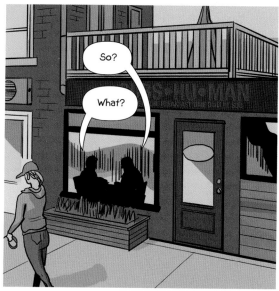

So?

What?

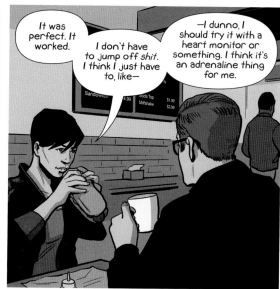

It was perfect. It worked.

I don't have to jump off *shit*. I think I just have to, like—

—I dunno, I should try it with a heart monitor or something. I think it's an adrenaline thing for me.

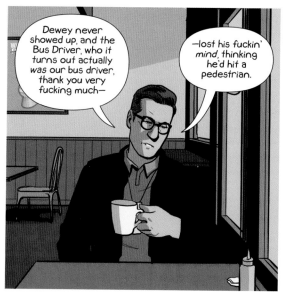

Dewey never showed up, and the Bus Driver, who it turns out actually *was* our bus driver, thank you very fucking much—

—lost his fuckin' *mind*, thinking he'd hit a pedestrian.

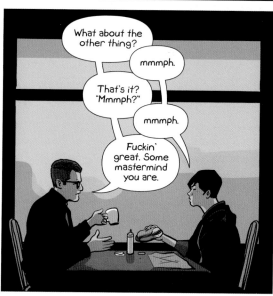

What about the other thing?

mmmph.

That's it? "Mmmph?"

mmmph.

Fuckin' great. Some mastermind you are.

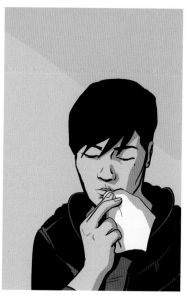

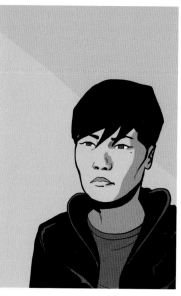

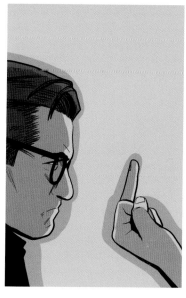

arriving sound
I miss you. Want to grab lunch sometime?
You gotta take that?
Bigger name on the other line?
No, yeah. Yeah. No. I...
Okay. Sure.
Great.
This is just fuckin' great.
Fuck my fucking life.
Hey, don't you have a *job* or—
Oh shit I'm gonna be late for work—

TWHIPPER
FACESITBOOK
instacram
Uh, let's see. I have a "George" next?
Hey, that's me.
That's us.
We keep having trouble with the Bluetooth pairing and I—
Oh holy shit.
George!
Oh my god! Jon!
It's great to see you!
You too!
Ron, this is Jon—oh my god, it rhymes, how funny is that—
—my husband Ron.
Ron, Jon and I dated in college for like—
—a semester or something, I don't know.
Best twelve weeks and spring break of my whole sophomore year. Nice to meet you.
So, married! That's amazing. That's great! Congratulations!
Oh who cares about me, what about you?
What have *you* been doing?
PENIS BAR
Uh...
BEST PICTURE

Oh, you know me.
This?
Just this?
...Shit, yeah, pretty much.
I worked in a bank for a while, but I fucked it up.
pink different.
vibrates
warms
lubes
the 2018
iPinky
Well, neat!
pink different.
You're the king of Cumworld!

I...
...I'm the king of Cumworld.
BEST PICTURE
BEST PICTURE

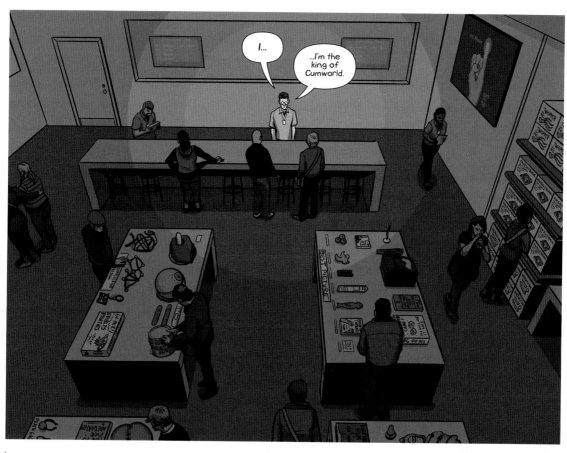

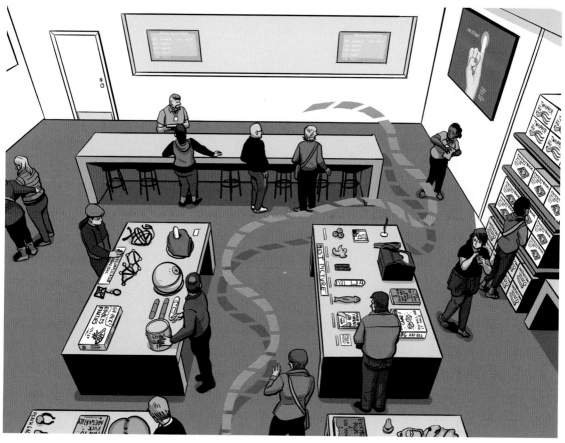

Hey, we need to talk.
Uh-oh.
Yeah, no, I know. Look...
The other night, at the club—
—You swore you were cool with it. You swore you wanted to go.
It was my idea! And I did.
Or at least I thought I did.
But I didn't, and I didn't want to be with anybody else, so I took off.
This is literally the first time a dude has said sorry for *not* hooking up with someone else.
Jon, I'm not gonna apologize for—
It's not that. It's not the club, it's not an open-relationship thing, it's not—
—This is hard. I'm sorry.
Never been able to articulate this before.
You're not doing such a great job now, but I'll bear with you.
Yeah, thanks.
I'm doing the best that I can.
I do this thing, see.
Or I used to, anyway—
—See, uh, my mom took off. When I was little.
And I was little, and I didn't understand adult relationship shit, so the only thing I could figure was...
...was what kind of kid was so bad his Mom had to leave?
Me.

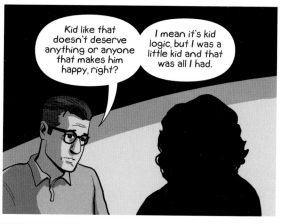

Kid like that doesn't deserve anything or anyone that makes him happy, right?

I mean it's kid logic, but I was a little kid and that was all I had.

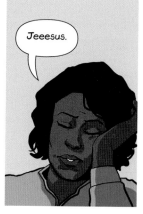

Jeeesus.

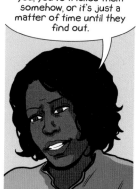

So then if someone likes you, you've tricked them somehow, or it's just a matter of time until they find out.

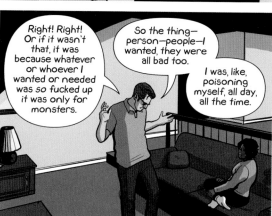

Right! Right! Or if it wasn't that, it was because whatever or whoever I wanted or needed was *so fucked up* it was only for monsters.

So the thing—person—people—I wanted, they were all bad too.

I was, like, poisoning myself, all day, all the time.

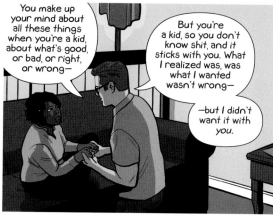

You make up your mind about all these things when you're a kid, about what's good, or bad, or right, or wrong—

But you're a kid, so you don't know shit, and it sticks with you. What I realized was, was what I wanted wasn't wrong—

—but I didn't want it with you.

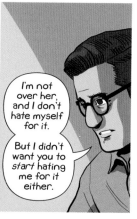

I'm not over her, and I don't hate myself for it.

But I didn't want you to *start* hating me for it either.

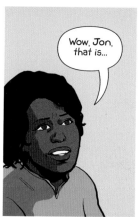

Wow, Jon, that is...

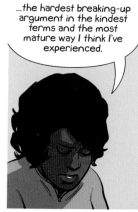

...the hardest breaking-up argument in the kindest terms and the most mature way I think I've experienced.

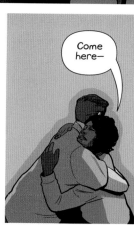

Come here—

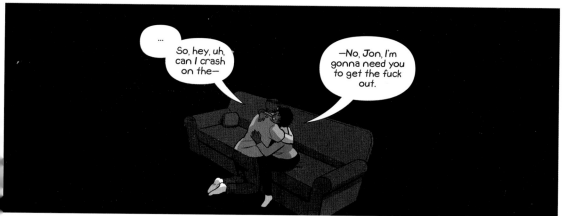

...

So, hey, uh, can I crash on the—

—No, Jon, I'm gonna need you to get the fuck out.

ROLL! YOU PRETTY THINGS
Are you fucking kidding me?
I haven't done this since I was a kid, and I'm not exactly in a place where health insurance is going to cover a broken ankle.
I mean, I'm all for the convivial break-up and post-relationship social interaction, but this seems fucking absurd.
I don't kid about the *Quad*.
Ever.
The ring is real, girl. Be good to her, and she'll be good to you.
Be good to her, she'll be good to you.
There you go. Easy.
And I appreciate keeping our relationship, post-"our relationship", convivial.
I honestly and earnestly have nothing but the utmost respect for your professional work.
In *either* of your fields.
Great. Now if only I could find a 22,000-RPM vibrator that wanted to fuck Jazmine for her mind and Ana for her body, I could die a happy woman.
That's the thing, though. It's not your past I can't get over—

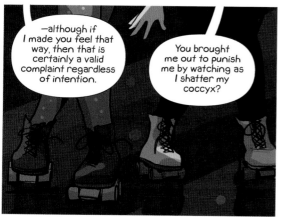

—although if I made you feel that way, then that is certainly a valid complaint regardless of intention.

You brought me out to punish me by watching as I shatter my coccyx?

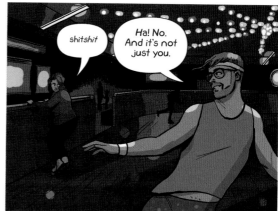

shit*shit*

Ha! No. And it's not just you.

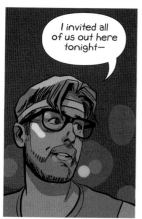

I invited all of us out here tonight—

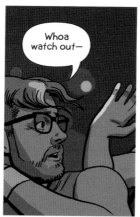

Whoa watch out—

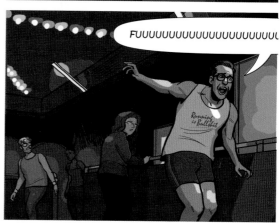

FUUUUUUUUUUUUUUUUUUUUUUU

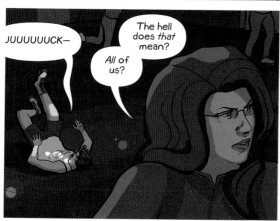

JUUUUUUUCK—

The hell does *that* mean?

All of us?

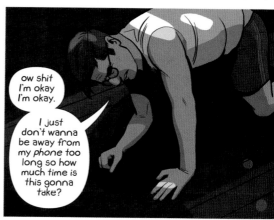

ow shit I'm okay I'm okay.

I just don't wanna be away from my *phone* too long so how much time is this gonna take?

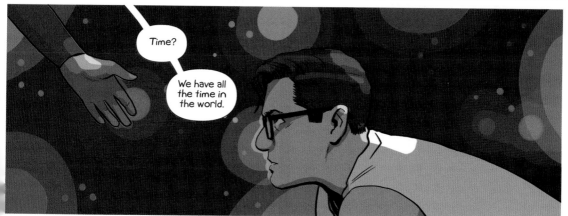

Time?

We have all the time in the world.

Let me help you.

Fuuuuuhhhhck YOU.

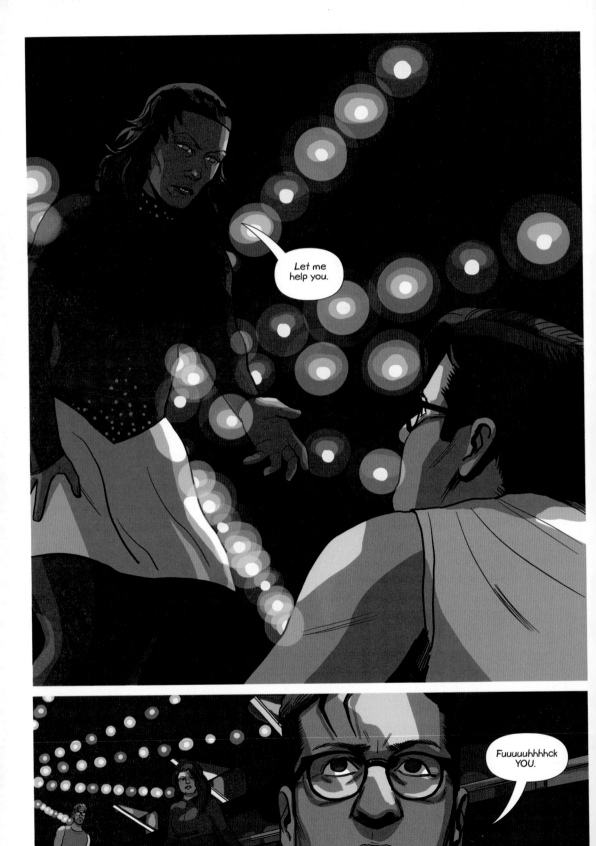

25
NO
TELL

The smell of it gets me.
The smell and the sound.
It's not a whiff of campfire or a chestnut-roasting-fireplace sort of fire.
This is fire where it shouldn't be.
It lets you know.

It's cotton and plastic, wiring and metal.
It's the scent of a life going up in ash.
And it sounds like the rumble of an oncoming train...
cough cough cough
cough ghaaak—

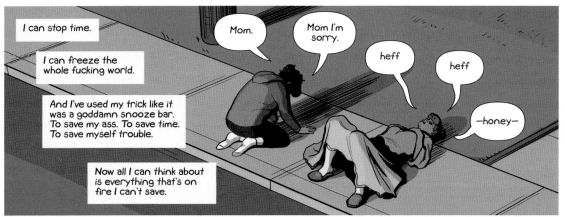

I can stop time.

I can freeze the whole fucking world.

And I've used my trick like it was a goddamn snooze bar. To save my ass. To save time. To save myself trouble.

Now all I can think about is everything that's on fire I can't save.

Mom.

Mom I'm sorry.

heff

heff

—honey—

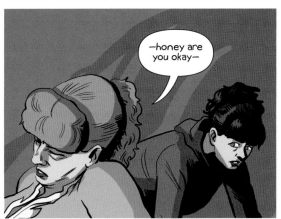

—honey are you okay—

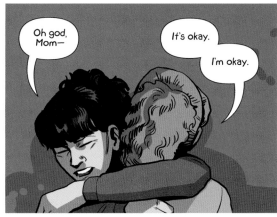

Oh god, Mom—

It's okay.

I'm okay.

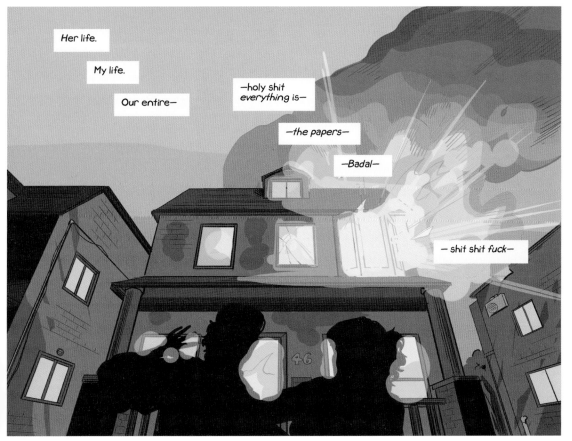

Her life.

My life.

Our entire—

—holy shit everything is—

—the papers—

—Badal—

— shit shit fuck—

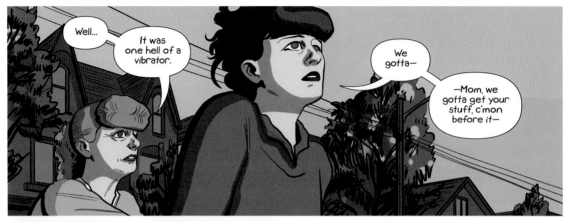

Well...

It was one hell of a vibrator.

We gotta—

—Mom, we gotta get your stuff, c'mon before it—

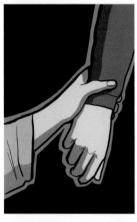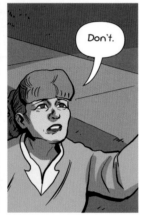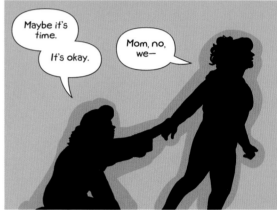

Don't.

Maybe it's time.

It's okay.

Mom, no, we—

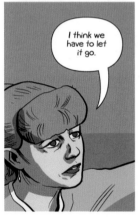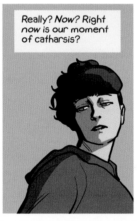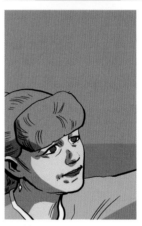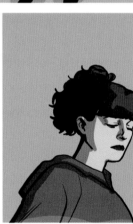

I think we have to let it go.

Really? *Now?* Right *now* is our moment of catharsis?

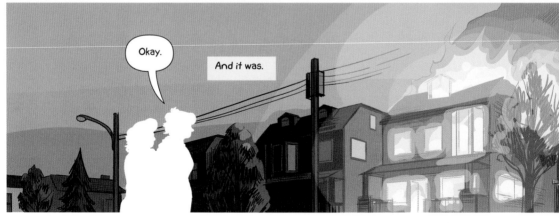

Okay.

And it was.

We sat there and watched.

Someone somewhere called the fire department, which was nice.

It seems like it took no time at all.

For the fire to eat everything.

For the firefighters to put it out.

But when they were gone...

...so was Mom's painstakingly reproduced museum that kept her life—

—our lives—

—frozen in amber.

I stand in the shower, beyond any and all rational time, eating up every drop of infinitely hot hotel water that comes.
I blow globs of black snot out of my nose until there's nothing left.
My skin glows like unto a thing of pink coral.
It's not enough.
Well if there's any water left anywhere in the world, I recommend using it all in the shower because holy crap it—
a locker like this, sometimes, hey, it's solid gold, and sometimes, hey, it's solid garbage, but then sometimes, hey—you just went and bought yourself a crime scene.
TONIGHT ON EVIDENCE WARS:

ksshhhhhhhhhhhhhhhh
hhhhhhhhhhh
h hhh
hh hh
h

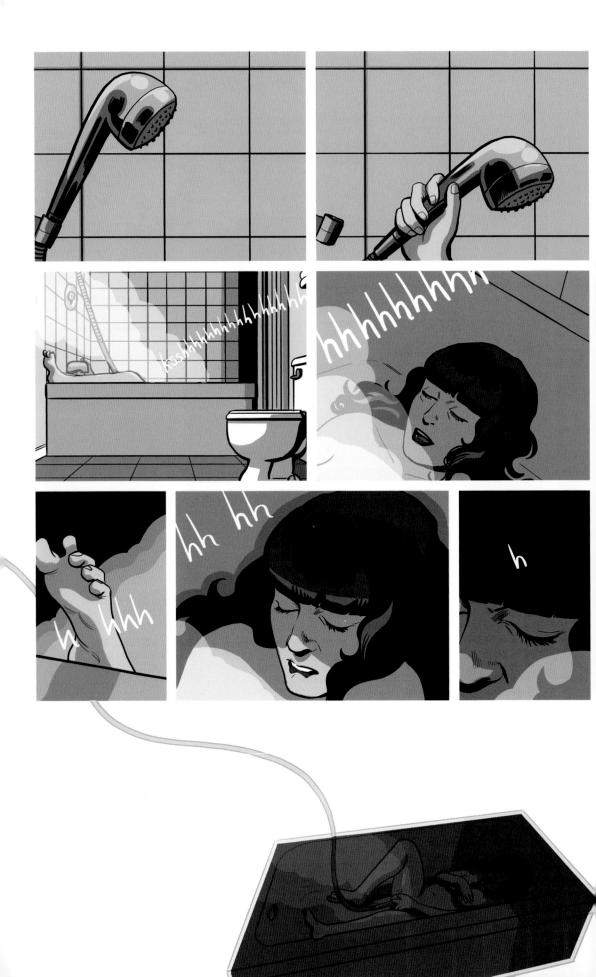

Whew!
That's better.
Hi.

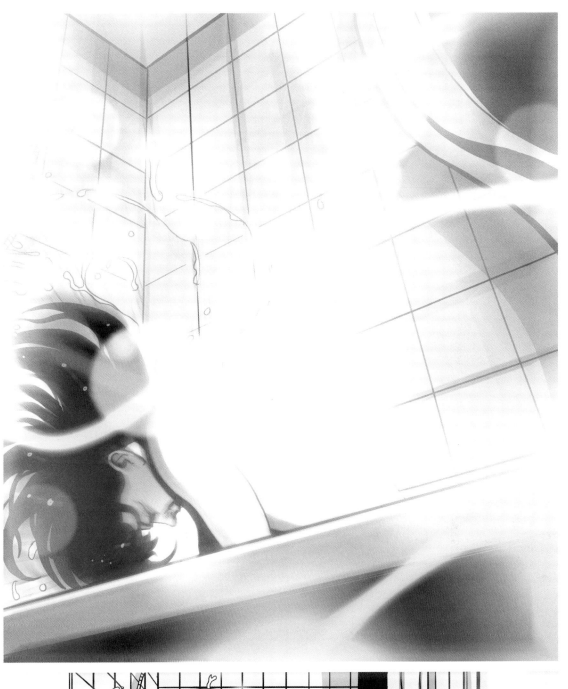

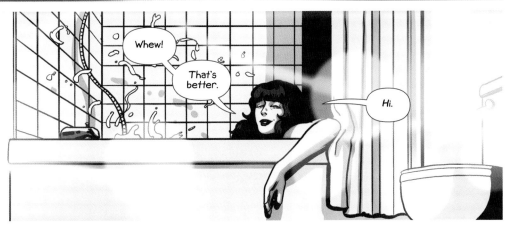

I just came harder than Rose Auerbach in a glove factory.
Feel like I can think again.
I started wondering "why?" Why the fire, why now, why this.
It's what we do, right? People, I mean.
Everything's gotta mean something.
Can't be random. Can't be chaos.
We want causes and effects, and try to find rational connections to—
—reinforce that two plus two still makes four.
Even if it's five plus 16, or 11 plus green or whatever.
IN AN EMERGENCY
Leave in a calm, orderly fashion, while thinking long and hard about why you decided to stay in a motel and not a hotel
surprisittyKNOCK KNOCK
Nothing just happefuckitty-FUCK!

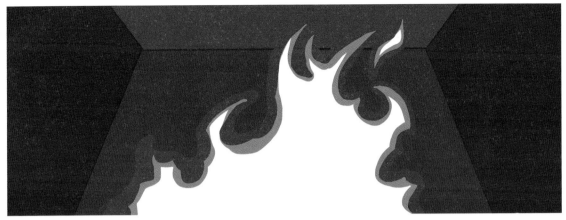

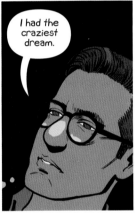
I had the craziest dream.

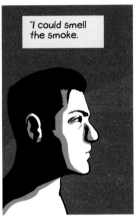
"I could smell the smoke.

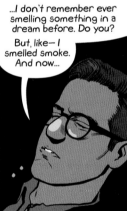
"I could feel heat on my face.

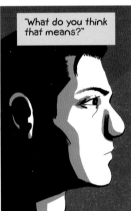
"What do you think that means?"

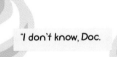
"I don't know, Doc.

"It's a dream.

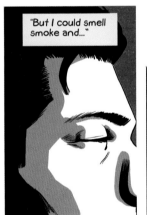
"But I could smell smoke and..."

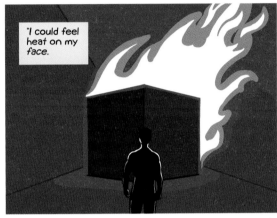
...I don't remember ever smelling something in a dream before. Do you?

But, like— I smelled smoke. And now...

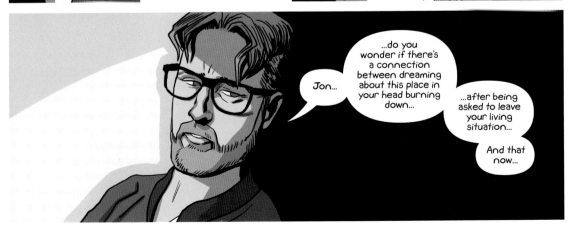
Jon...

...do you wonder if there's a connection between dreaming about this place in your head burning down...

...after being asked to leave your living situation...

And that now...

...you're living in your car?
Running is Bullshit
Doc, the problem wasn't the place.
The problem was *me*.
Jon.
Doc.
Why are you here, man? I'm telling you, I've had an experience here, a real, y'know.
A thing.
And now you live.
In a car.
And *you* are hanging out with *her*.
THE QUEEN'S PUDD
I mean, what the *fuck*, man?

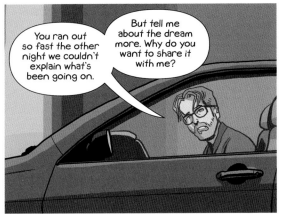

You ran out so fast the other night we couldn't explain what's been going on.

But tell me about the dream more. Why do you want to share it with me?

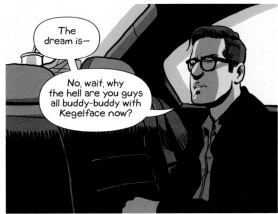

The dream is—

No, wait, why the hell are you guys all buddy-buddy with Kegelface now?

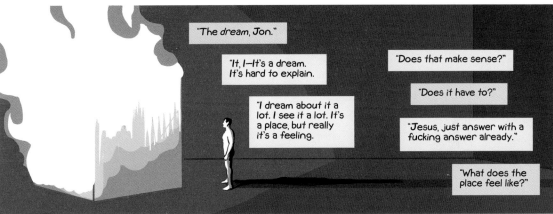

"The *dream*, Jon."

"It, I—It's a dream. It's hard to explain.

"I dream about it a lot. I see it a lot. It's a place, but really it's a feeling.

"Does that make sense?"

"Does it have to?"

"Jesus, just answer with a fucking answer already."

"What does the place feel like?"

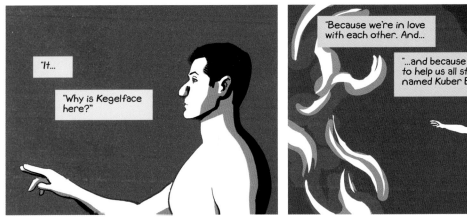

"It...

"Why is Kegelface here?"

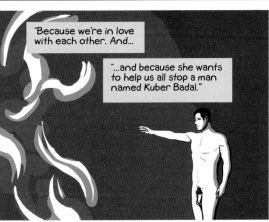

"Because we're in love with each other. And...

"...and because she wants to help us all stop a man named Kuber Badal."

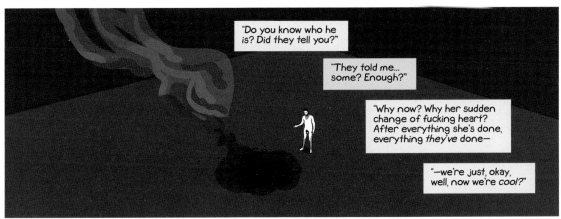

"Do you know who he is? Did they tell you?"

"They told me... some? Enough?"

"Why now? Why her sudden change of fucking heart? After everything she's done, everything *they've* done—

"—we're just, okay, well, now we're *cool*?"

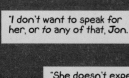 "I don't want to speak for her, or to any of that, Jon.

"She doesn't expect to be forgiven.

"She explained why she chose to do what she did, and how she came to realize she was wrong.

"And now she wants to make amends by doing the right thing.

"And she hopes that, over time, if she keeps doing the right thing...

"...Jon, I think you're right.

"'The place wasn't the problem.' You know what I mean?"

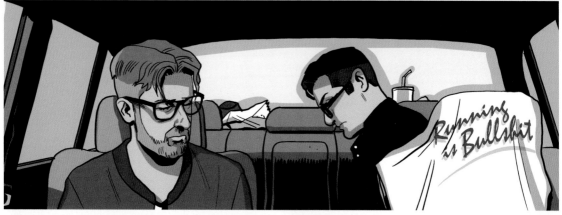

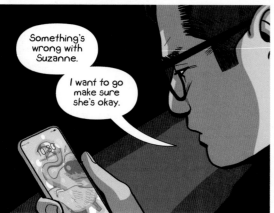 Something's wrong with Suzanne.

I want to go make sure she's okay.

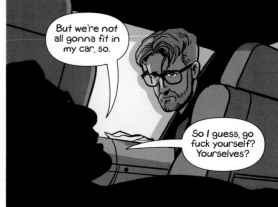 But we're not all gonna fit in my car, so.

So I guess, go fuck yourself? Yourselves?

bloorp
bloorrrrp
Oh no, fuck that—
That guy hit me in the face with a goddamn dildo! He—
Hey guys!
Sorry we're late.
And I'm real sorry about hitting you with that dildo that one time.
OUT OF SERVICE
Aww, where's your special lady-friend, buddy?
Are we going to pick her up next?

Boy, I, uh...
...sure wish you'd be in a seat instead of standing there.
It's not safe.
Was it safe when you zapped me with a VadgeVolt Tangtaser 6900 or smacked me in the face with a dildo, you busdriving fuck?
Beg pardon?
What now?
Turn-left-on-Globbracrobbo-Seetee.
Left on Alvarado Ct.
So, her mom's place, huh?
Is she—
Are they—
You can ask her when you see her, Jon.
And she can tell you all about it if she so chooses.
Oh, shit—
ATE ASS
APPLETOWN TRANSIT
ENTERPRISE
ASSOCIATED

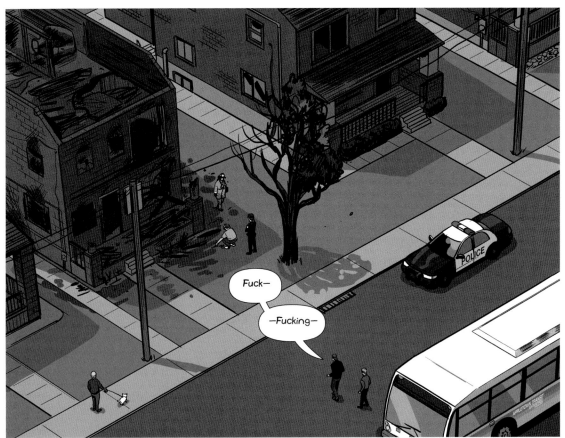

Fuck—

—Fucking—

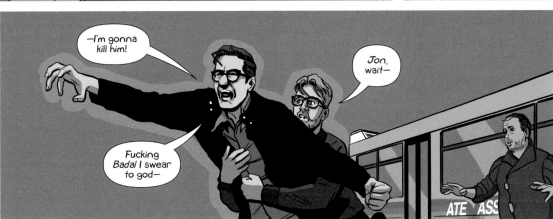

—I'm gonna kill him!

Jon, wait—

Fucking *Badal* I swear to god—

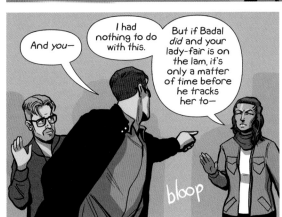

And you—

I had nothing to do with this.

But if Badal *did* and your lady-fair is on the lam, it's only a matter of time before he tracks her to—

bloop

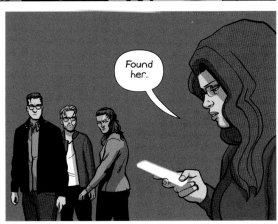

Found her.

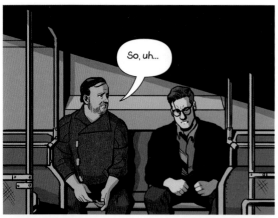

So, uh...

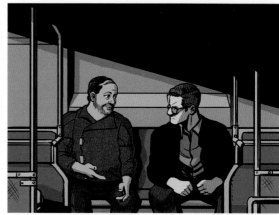

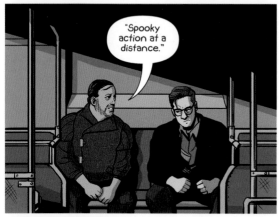

"Spooky action at a distance."

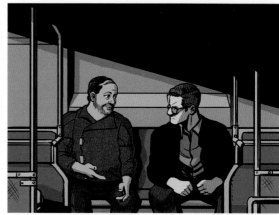

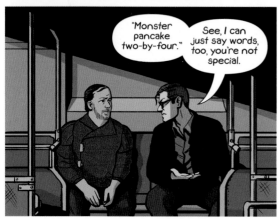

"Monster pancake two-by-four."

See, I can just say words, too, you're not special.

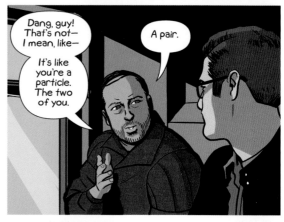

Dang, guy! That's not— I mean, like—

It's like you're a particle. The two of you.

A pair.

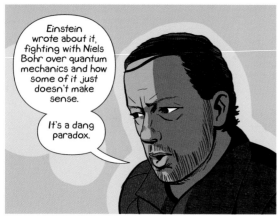

Einstein wrote about it, fighting with Niels Bohr over quantum mechanics and how some of it just doesn't make sense.

It's a dang paradox.

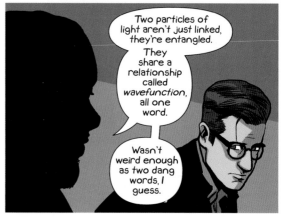

Two particles of light aren't just linked, they're entangled.

They share a relationship called *wavefunction*, all one word.

Wasn't weird enough as two dang words, I guess.

The two particles, the photons, see, become so tied together—
—that what happens to one influences the other.
No matter how far apart they are.
And it happens instantly, faster than light maybe, so it was a whole thing.
They're still trying to figure it out.
You get into issues of locality, freedom-of-choice loopholes, super-determinism—
—none of it changes the heart of the thing, though, the *Spukhafte Fernwirkung* of it all.
It's *weird*.
A thing happens to a thing over here— it happens to a thing over there.
You dream about a fire. A house burns down. *Her* house.
I'm saying, the dang space between you two doesn't matter.
You're entwined.
...Are you saying I burned down my girlfriend's house in my sleep?
Gosh, no!
That'd be *crazy*.

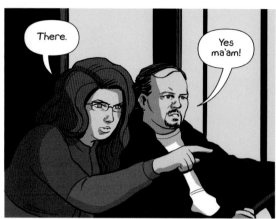

There.

Yes ma'am!

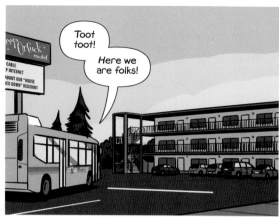

Toot toot!

Here we are folks!

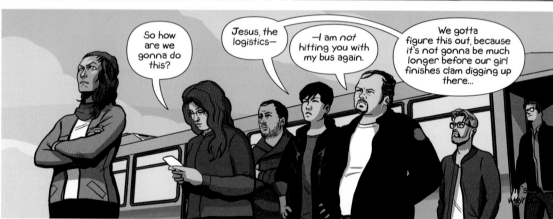

So how are we gonna do this?

Jesus, the logistics—

—I am *not* hitting you with my bus again.

We gotta figure this out, because it's not gonna be much longer before our girl finishes clam digging up there...

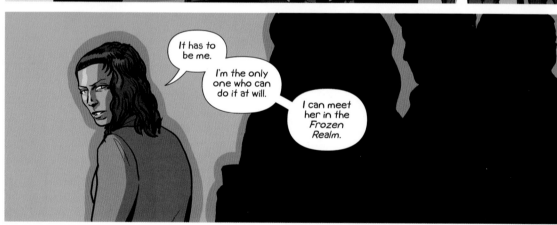

It has to be me.

I'm the only one who can do it at will.

I can meet her in the *Frozen Realm.*

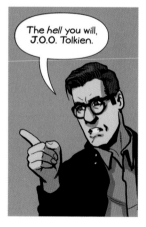

The *hell* you will, J.O.O. Tolkien.

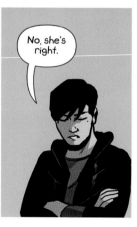

No, she's right.

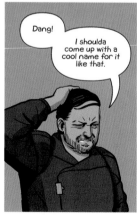

Dang!

I shoulda come up with a cool name for it like that.

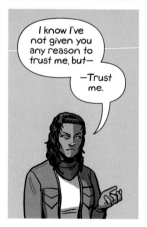

I know I've not given you any reason to trust me, but—

—Trust me.

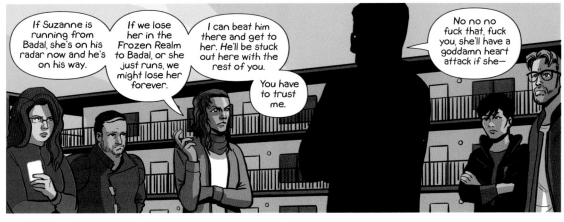

If Suzanne is running from Badal, she's on his radar now and he's on his way.

If we lose her in the Frozen Realm to Badal, or she just runs, we might lose her forever.

I can beat him there and get to her. He'll be stuck out here with the rest of you.

You have to trust me.

No no no fuck that, fuck you, she'll have a goddamn heart attack if she—

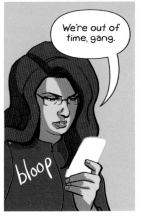

We're out of time, gang.

bloop

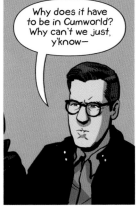

Why does it have to be in Cumworld? Why can't we just, y'know—

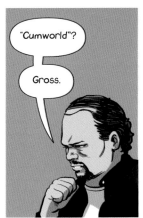

"Cumworld"?

Gross.

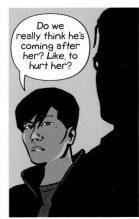

Do we really think he's coming after her? Like, to hurt her?

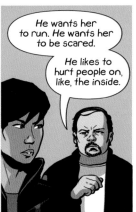

He wants her to run. He wants her to be scared.

He likes to hurt people on, like, the inside.

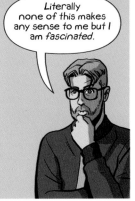

Literally none of this makes any sense to me but I am *fascinated*.

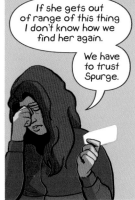

If she gets out of range of this thing I don't know how we find her again.

We have to trust Spurge.

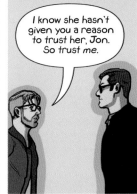

I know she hasn't given you a reason to trust her, Jon. So trust *me*.

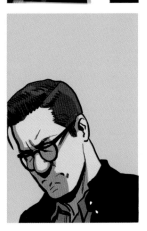

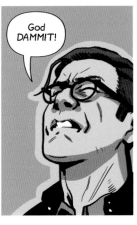

God DAMMIT!

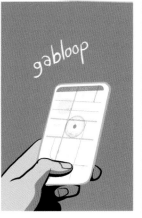

gabloop

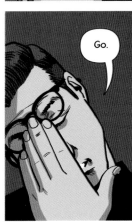

Go.

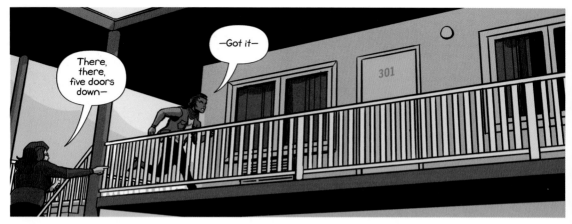

There, there, five doors down—

—Got it—

301

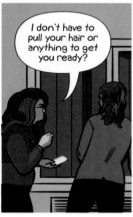

I don't have to pull your hair or anything to get you ready?

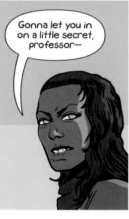

Gonna let you in on a little secret, professor—

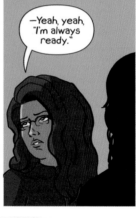

—Yeah, yeah, "I'm always ready."

I was going to say that contrary to what's currently à la mode avec porn, I don't respond erotically to having my hair pulled.

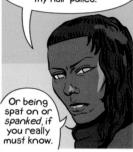

Or being spat on or *spanked*, if you really must know.

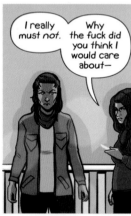

I really must *not*. Why the fuck did you think I would care about—

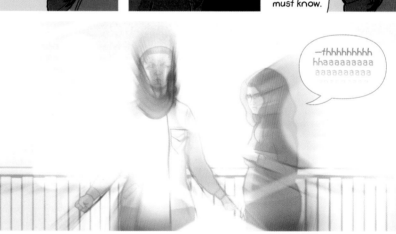

—thhhhhhhh hhaaaaaaaaa aaaaaaaaaa

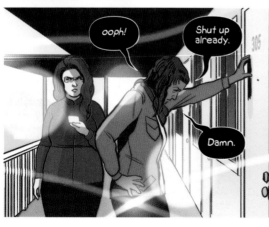

ooph!

Shut up already.

305

Damn.

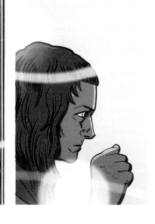

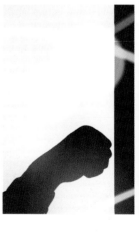

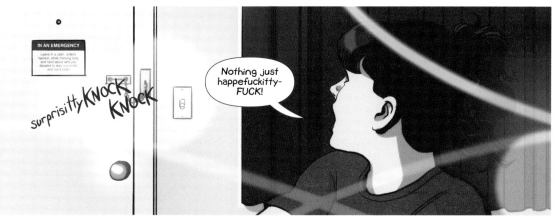

Nothing just happefuckitty-FUCK!

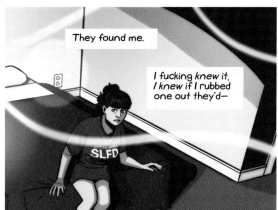

They found me.

I fucking *knew* it, I *knew* if I rubbed one out they'd—

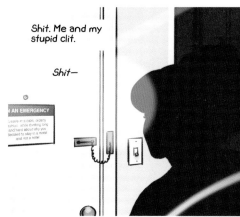

Shit. Me and my stupid clit.

Shit—

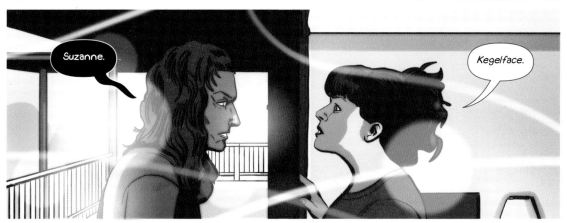

Suzanne.

Kegelface.

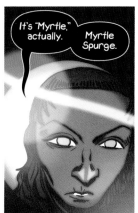

It's "Myrtle," actually. Myrtle Spurge.

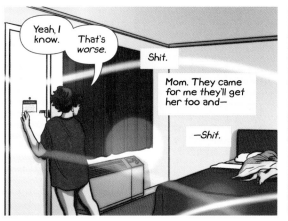

Yeah, I know.

That's *worse*.

Shit.

Mom. They came for me they'll get her too and—

—*Shit.*

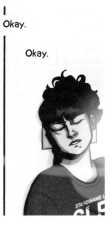

Okay.

Okay.

305
ckc
Suzanne, I—
305
klatch
305
unchain unchain unchain
I—
FUCK YOU—!!
304

—Suzanne wait—
—fuck you FUCK YOU—
—Come after me? *Fine!*
Come for my *mother?*
Her *home?!?*
FUCK!
YOU!
I was *fine!* I was *alone!*
We weren't doing *anything* to you—!!
—*Suzanne* look—
—Look who I'm *with*—

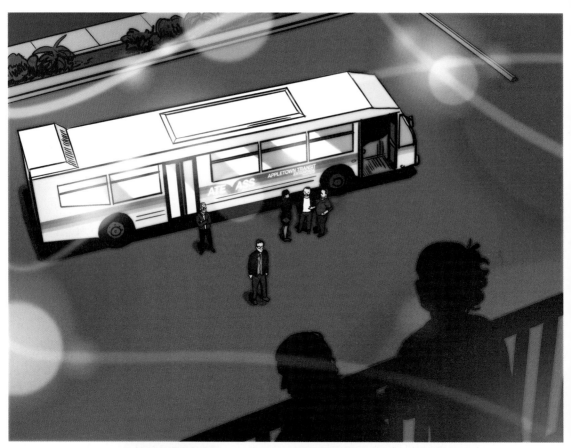

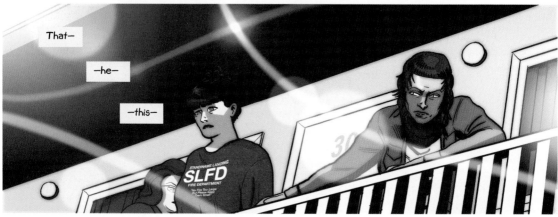

That—

—he—

—this—

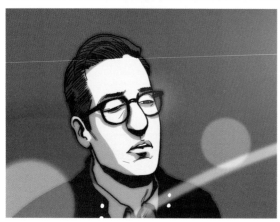

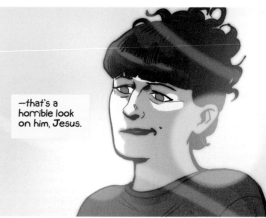

—that's a horrible look on him, Jesus.

This—

This fuckin'—

SLFD

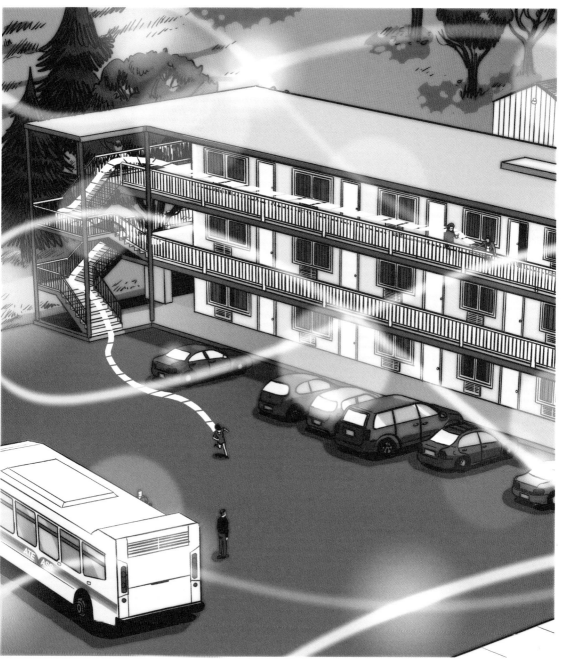

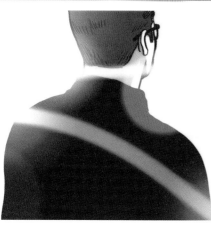

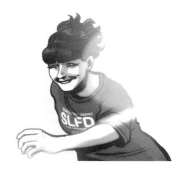

This fuckin' guy.

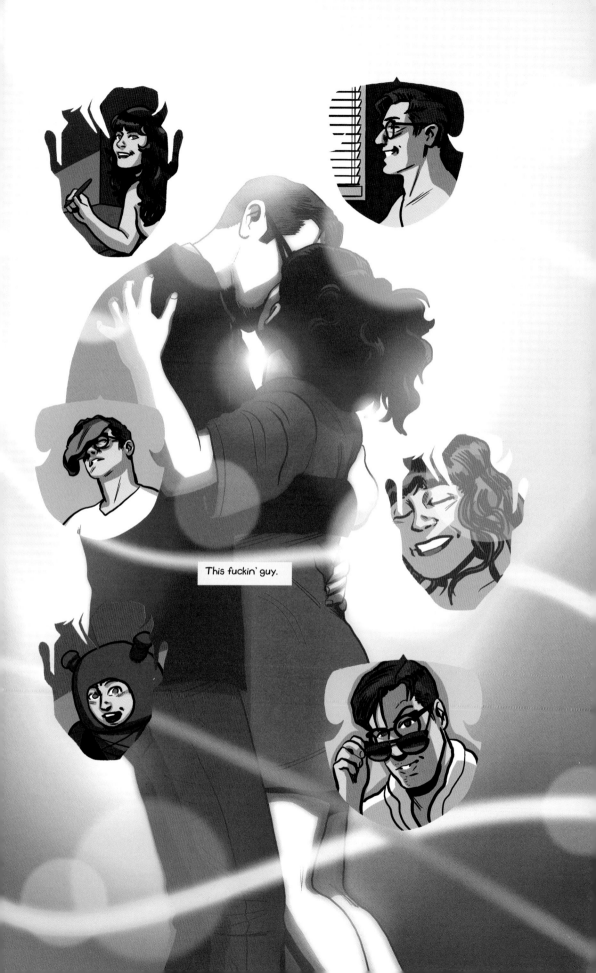

I don't—
How did—
—I don't care.
I mean, I was, I was waiting and then...
...oh fuck it—

Hey you.
Hey you.
Is—
—Is this real?
I mean, this is really happening?
I don't know...?
Suzanne, I'm sorry. I'm sorry.
I am so—

Yes. Good. No.
I know.
And you should be, but first—
—First, I—
SLFD
I—
SLFD
—I liiiiiike you...?
...A lot?
Little soon, isn't it?

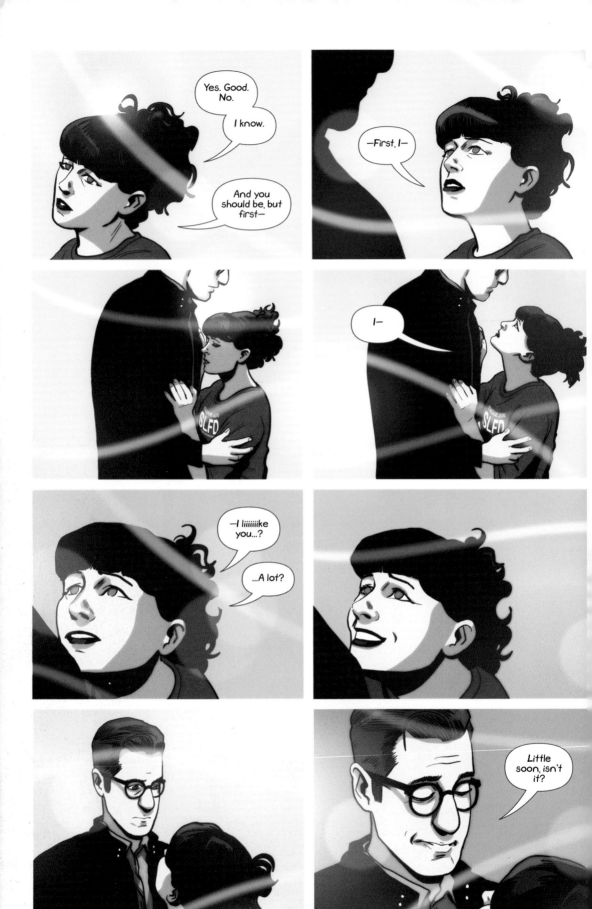

SleepOrfuck motel
FRE3 CABLE
CHEEP INTERNET
ASK ABOUT OUR "HOU5E BURNED DOWN" DISCOUNT
Only Sleeping
Fuck you.

Matt Fraction is the author
of many bios for Matt Fraction
appearing in books such as
*ODY-C, Satellite Sam,
Casanova,* and very soon
Adventureman! and *November.*

Chip Zdarsky can't escape the feeling
that bio pages are future obituaries so
let's just say he did a lot of charity
work and fucked like a champ.

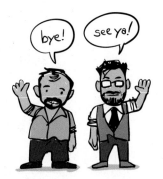